William Burnet Wright

The World to Come

William Burnet Wright

The World to Come

ISBN/EAN: 9783337120214

Printed in Europe, USA, Canada, Australia, Japan

Cover: Foto ©Lupo / pixelio.de

More available books at **www.hansebooks.com**

THE WORLD TO COME

BY

WILLIAM BURNET WRIGHT
AUTHOR OF "ANCIENT CITIES"

BOSTON AND NEW YORK
HOUGHTON, MIFFLIN AND COMPANY
The Riverside Press, Cambridge
1887

The Riverside Press, Cambridge:
Electrotyped and Printed by H. O. Houghton & Co.

PREFACE.

WHEN the earthly grandeur of Israel had vanished and the vast majority of Israelites were exiles, an inspired teacher wrote the Epistle to the Hebrews. It cheered them with the hope that their wanderings would end in a city fairer than the old Jerusalem had ever been; a city in which righteousness should rule, love prevail, peace and joy be the portion of every citizen. Other parts of the New Testament offer to all men the same radiant hope, and assure us that though the desired place is always at hand, it can be entered only by those who are "born from above," and is discerned by those alone whose eyes Christ has opened to see things which, though they have been present from the foundation of the world, have been hidden from men's eyes, because men "having eyes see not the things belonging to their peace."

That city, the author of the Epistle to the Hebrews named in the phrase selected for the title of this book, " The World to Come."

For its coming all men hope. For its coming all good men toil. Into it Mr. Herbert Spencer and Mr. Henry George are endeavoring earnestly and honestly to lead us by different but, I think, by equally mistaken roads. It will never be reached except by the steep and narrow way to which the Master pointed.

The vague but universal expectation of the world which is to come is expressed in the text of the opening paper. The rate of our approach toward what all desire is in some degree measured by the history of Christmas with which the volume closes.

That we can all wish each other " A Happy New Year " implies the general hope of a future in which there shall be no more sighing.

The history of Christmas may serve to show that so much of progress toward that future as can be measured by the gradual transformation of the Roman Saturnalia into the German festival has consumed about fifteen hundred years.

Most of us already spend one three-hundred-and-sixty-fifth part of our time in an atmosphere distinctively Christian; in a world where the true business of life is practically conceded to be — what our Saviour affirms that it is — not getting for ourselves, but giving to others. Already during one day of each year the Holy Spirit is poured out upon all flesh, as if God compelled us to be Christians for a little while, in order that we might know by actual experience how good and pleasant it is to enter into the joy of our Lord, and continue Christians by our own choice the remainder of the time.

How soon the lesson will be learned effectually and all our time redeemed by Him who declares that it is more blessed to give than to receive, the reader can calculate as easily as I. We know that God is long-suffering and marvellously patient.

What external changes the future may bring to increase human felicity I do not know. Whatever they may be, I cannot think them essential to our happiness while I hear one who is the Truth asking for those He loves — even while He accepts the cup which He pleads with a great agony to have pass from Him, and faces the trials which marked Him as the Man of Sorrows — "that they may have my joy fulfilled in themselves." But it seems to me supremely important for every man to understand that he can reach heaven only by walking the steep and narrow way, and that the essential conditions of all joy are deliverance from those sins and possession of those virtues, of which such as I have oftenest needed to remind myself and my brethren are in this book brought to view.

In the selection of sermons I have carefully avoided all which treat of questions in debate, and have chosen those which depend for such force as they have upon principles acknowledged by the universal Christian conscience as true. In other words, the following pages deal not with the ephemeral phases of human speculation, but with the permanent elements of human nature.

The tinge of local coloring in the Memorial of Franklin Snow comes from the fact that it — as were all the utterances in this book — was spoken in Berkeley Street Church, Boston, of which Mr. Snow was at the time of his death a deacon, and the speaker was the pastor. The closing paper is not a sermon, but a familiar talk given to the young people of the same Church at a certain Christmas festival which many of them will remember, and afterwards repeated to larger audiences in different parts of New England. I hope it may strengthen the reader's conviction that the stones for the strong foundations of the New Jerusalem and for the walls which " are both great and high " must be quarried from the Mountain of the Beatitudes;

for only he "who heareth these sayings of mine and doeth them" builds for himself a home which neither storm nor flood can sweep away.

CONTENTS.

		PAGE
I.	A Happy New Year	1
II.	The Model Church	15
III.	Teach us to Pray	32
IV.	The Keys of the Kingdom	45
V.	Spiritual Ploughing	59
VI.	Jericho	74
VII.	Gideon's Men	88
VIII.	Self-Pity: Saul in the Witch's Cave	100
IX.	Samson: Self-Deception	112
X.	To Parents	124
XI.	Saving Faith	139
XII.	Franklin Snow	149
XIII.	What Must I do to be Saved?	177
XIV.	What has God done to Save Me?	194
XV.	The Missionary Spirit	209
XVI.	Easter: Transfiguration	222
XVII.	Flower Sunday	233
XVIII.	Decoration Day	241
XIX.	Harvest Sunday	253
XX.	Christmas	267

THE WORLD TO COME.

I.

A HAPPY NEW YEAR.

"I wish you a happy New Year."

I MUST take a little time to give you the chapter and verse of the text, because I have heard it from so many lips, and seen it in so many faces, of which the Concordance issued in heaven has not yet been republished upon earth.

The last day of the old year was not altogether bright to me. Clouds were thick when it dawned. Within fourteen days I had ministered at fourteen funerals. Early in the afternoon I was called to visit a mother, two of whose children had been buried the week before, and who was herself thought to be dying. A friend stopped me on the doorstep to ask if I could officiate at another funeral the next afternoon. I was beginning to feel that this is a bad world, with too much trouble in it. For a minister, I know, and for you, I think, it is worse to doubt any of those words of the Master in which He said, "Blessed are they that mourn," than to doubt the things which men have put in the creeds about the Trinity, or the Atonement, or endless punishment. And how bad it is to question the latter, any of the theology books will tell you. A consciousness of the sorrowfulness of life was creeping like mildew over me, as I passed into a neighborhood where only poor people live. There the stores are dingy, and most of them are in cellars. Baskets of coal, painfully small, and puny bunches of fagots are for sale upon the sidewalk. The day was bitterly cold. On such days few sights are more pitiful than these tiny morsels of fuel, which the poor buy when they can afford them. As I crossed the broad street which divides your neighborhood from this section, I heard my name called. A bright face shone, a cheery voice exclaimed, "I wish you a happy New Year." We shook hands, and a star seemed to be struggling through the clouds. Not everybody was crying.

I passed on. A mother — a member of our church; two sick children; yet the single room in which they all lived together seemed empty to her, because within a fortnight two other children had been carried from it, never to return. The poor love their children perhaps the more because they have so little else to love. The poor woman finds in her babe all of light and laughter that she has; all that books, flowers, amusement, society, travel, and children, give to you. This mother had come near following her loved little ones, the night before. She was very weak. But she had strength enough to say these three things: "I have slept a whole hour, and I feel so rested." "I never thought of it in that way before. He had not where to lay his head, and I have a good bed to lie upon." And, as I came away, "I wish you a happy New Year." The clouds were growing thin.

Then Miss B—— wanted me to visit an aged Scotch woman, who had asked to see me because, seven years ago, when she was still in the old country, I buried her daughter. She lives in a cellar. She is old, and her brogue was hard for me to understand. She had rheumatism, and a pleurisy pain in her side, and a few weeks ago she fell upon the stairs, and the jar was terrible. She had never seen me before, but when my name was spoken, memories came. Hers was the familiar story, — " Son that never let her want for anything when he had it to give; out of work now. The landlord was not pressing for the three weeks' rent, and Jamie was promised a long job come the New Year; and she had had a splendid cup o' tea the morn, and there was eneuch for the morrow; and a gude woman cam at the gloamin', to cook the meal and tidy a bit. But times her head gaed woad, and she forgot the endin' o' the psaulms, tho' gen the prayers cam short and she could na mind the endin', perhaps the Lord mindid a' the same! And wad I pray." " Yes! But do not try to kneel, for it hurts you!" " But it's little eneuch to kneel before Him!" So we helped her off the bed, and after prayers we helped her back upon it. And " God be wie ye, sir," she said, as she wished me " a happy New Year."

The clouds were almost gone as I entered the room of a dear friend who has been confined some weeks to her chamber, and heard her say: " I will not remind you that you have not been in my house for a year, because I am so glad to see you and to wish you ' a happy New Year.'"

The sky was clear when at last I joined some of you in the rooms below, and saw sixty or seventy tots of children, dressed in their best, and saw you trying with all your skill to make them happy. It takes so little to make children happy! Even the three with pinched faces who at first shrunk apart, and would not join in the games because their clothes were shabby, soon began to look eager and delighted. I never loved our superintendent and our deacons so well, as while I saw them racing with the gleeful babies, and so becoming little children after the manner of those who enter the kingdom of God. "Let's sing now," they said. " What shall we sing?" Sing " Christ was shined in Bethlehem!" cried a tiny tot of rapturous humanity.

You should have seen their eyes dilate, heard their shouts of ecstasy when a kind friend turned eggs into rabbits, and brought doves out of tin cans. Feeling richer than Crœsus with his gold, each little one was led home at seven with his orange and his bag of peanuts.

It takes so little to make children happy, and yet they are so often unhappy!

In the evening the older members of the

Sunday-school convened, and so sweet a celebration, so joyous and so gracious a meeting I have rarely seen. All seemed to rejoice, as if they knew whose hand would lead them safely through the unexplored and tangled paths of the future, and therefore felt, "Nothing can hurt us, nothing can make us afraid, for He will be with us always, and none can pluck us out of his hand."

It was half past nine when an esteemed friend took both my hands and said: "It is time, I think, to wish you a happy New Year." He little thought, perhaps none of you thought, how mightily you were working to make my New Year happy.

Three children went home with me, and each of them declared they had never had so good a time before. The next morning, before my eyelids opened, a patter of little feet, a shout, a kiss, a chorus of "Happy New Year, papa!" mingled with this radiant refrain, "I love to go to church where they have real doves."

The text is one of those utterances. Which one I cannot quite tell, and perhaps it does not matter, for all of them may be found in the Lamb's Book of Life.

1. I remark; though the words of the text

do not occur in the Bible, they are none the less inspired. Every one who has sincerely uttered them has spoken by inspiration of the Holy Spirit. It is God who makes you love your neighbor, and I shall do a worthy work to-day, if I can make you realize that the fervent love you feel for your friends and your families comes from Him whose name is Love. Could any other than God's Spirit inspire a young lady, elegantly dressed, to plunge through carts and cars across the muddy street, risking her comfort and her toilet, just from loving-kindness, to wish me a-happy New Year? Was it not God's Spirit that, checking the envy so common to us all, moved a sick woman, old, suffering, in rags, in a cellar, with no money and few friends, her rent unpaid, rheumatism in her bones and chilblains in her feet, to look at me, sleek, well-dressed, well-fed, glowing with health, and sincerely wish me " a happy New Year"? But for God, she would have been eying this gold watch-chain and saying, "It might be sold for much, and given to the poor!" But for God, she would be thinking, "Is he better than I, who read my Bible and say my prayers every day, and have not a cent with which to bless myself?" Was it not the Spirit of God which said, "I will not remind you that you have not been to see me for a year, because I am so glad to see you and to wish you a happy New Year"?

And was it not God's Spirit that guided old and young in the rooms below, to enact the same greeting in such a way that I went home feeling so full of gladness that to sleep seemed to squander joy?

Friends, whoso loveth is born of God. He that loveth his brother, whom he hath seen, is growing in the love of God, whom he hath not seen. For this New Year's greeting is in fact the exact benediction which Heaven spoke upon Earth over the cradle of Christ. It is the prayer which Jesus uttered for his own when He asked that they might be one; and the fulfilment of the radiant permission, "Enter into my joy."

2. My hope dilates and my courage grows because so many have sincerely said, "I wish you a happy New Year." From millions of hearts this great psalm of the new life has ascended. Some have spoken insincerely. In some the lips have belied the heart. There are pharisees of fashion as there are pharisees of religion. But oftenest far the words have been genuine. How earnestly

do parents desire a happy New Year for their children; friends for their friends. For how many of those that mourn, and of those who are poor, has the wish been honestly felt, " May they have a more cheerful future." How much true charity have these Christmas holidays beheld.

If the recording angels are as careful of good words as of idle ones, — and who can question that they are — they have been busy this past week over the Lamb's Book. When the Lion of the tribe of Judah prevails to open it for us, we shall read many things we have not written in our notebooks; we shall miss much that we have printed in our largest type.

" *He hath built us a synagogue* " may have been entered on high. But

SHE HATH CAST IN TWO MITES

all eyes shall see.

Remember these kind greetings are prayers. God himself has inspired them, and they show that He is wishing us a happy New Year.

3. God has in reserve for every one of us, this coming year, something better than we can ask or think. It is most appropriate

for us to begin the year at the communion table. For the happiness of our future depends upon our communion with Him at whose right hand are pleasures forevermore. They who walk with God shall be happy; they who live nearest God shall be happiest.

In all the realms of life you shall find no creatures joyful save such as obey the laws of their being. God so wishes all his creatures to be glad, that He has shown to each of them the things belonging to their peace. To the brutes by instinct, to us by reason and by revelation, He has revealed the conditions under which alone we can be glad. These conditions we call laws, and talk about them as if they were arbitrary requirements of our Father; as if He were a king who makes decrees for his own pleasure, and punishes those who disobey them. But God's Statute Book declares, "There is no peace for the wicked." God himself could not find that which "is not." "Wisdom's ways are ways of pleasantness, and all her paths are peace." "I wish you a happy New Year for time, for eternity!" This is the meaning of the law which warns, of the gospel which woos. To wish you all "a happy New Year" is to wish you all Christians.

Let the year that is past be our compass for the year that is passing. From some of you money has gone; from some friends have been taken; some have been sick; some have been slandered; some have failed in their undertakings; some have worked till they are very weary; some have lost heart and hope and faith. As the past has been, the future will be, except for the changes within us. Do you need a stay that is not rooted in the ground? A support that earthquakes cannot throw down? The things we have most lamented, it may be, have been God's best gifts to us. Is there green grass in the desert? Do flowers blossom there? Are fruits ripened above its sands? Yet there the sun always shines. There clouds never come. There the blue sky bends always over all. And no frost chills the air. But the only fruits of its perpetual radiance are the bleaching bones of camels and men, who have tried in vain to cross it. There can be no rain where clouds never come, for He, by whom in the beginning all things were made that were made, wrote in the silent ground what He read aloud to his suffering children when He stood upon the mount, "Blessed are they that mourn."

4. My friends, if we begin this year seeking our own ends and not God's, we shall be as children who enter school not to learn and grow wise by their teacher's wisdom, but to idle or to play. For them there shall be pain and punishment and tears. No love sweetens their daily work, and at the end no dear assurance of rest and full contentment, — "Well done, good and faithful."

Remember, whatever your plans may be, God has something for you to do. You may not yet see what it is. Then wait upon Him and He will show you. His will is not only that you may grow rich; He may not mean you to succeed in the things you propose for yourself. He means you to become a truer, wiser, stronger man; more just, more brave, more loving. That is surely his first purpose for you. Is it your first purpose for yourself? If you do that, whatever else may come of loss or trouble, will you feel sure that you have not failed, though all the newspapers in the land and all the commercial registers write you down a bankrupt? If not, you are not fit to do business in God's world.

There are two natures in every one of us, fighting for the mastery: a higher and a lower. If we put the sceptre in the hands of impulse, and take counsel only of our wishes and our passions, we shall have torment enough. A beast is a good thing to drive; but alas for the man who is driven by a beast! If we crown principle and take counsel of God we shall have his peace that passeth understanding.

When spring comes I shall look upon the fields. Here and there, in early April, perhaps I shall find one green, and growing daily greener. No blade in it that breaks the ground shall be disturbed. No flower that peers shall be uprooted. That field shall keep all its growths, no sharp share shall wound its breast, and I shall know the farmer has given it over to lie barren. It will bear no harvest either of beauty or of fruit. "Ephraim is joined to his idols, let him alone." God will not hurt us when we are past being helped by pain.

Other fields I shall see, cut with sharp shares, pounded and pierced by harrows; every blade that peers toward heaven uprooted, every flower torn up, till the ground seems sterile as desert wastes. In such fields I shall look for harvests. There, in due time, I shall find flowers, fruits, grain. When ye are stripped and scarred and scourged, listen to the Lord's voice; He is saying, "All this is because I wish you a happy New Year!"

Does the future mean to us earth or heaven? A few months and the new year shall be old. A few years, and all years shall be ended. In a moment, in the twinkling of an eye, for each of us mortality shall be swallowed up of life.

Let us realize that we are immortal. Let us remember that the themes we ponder here on this day are infinitely more momentous than those presented by the counting-room, the kitchen, or the parlor. Let us give them their lawful sovereignty. Let us live as becometh immortal sons of God, loving each other because God hath loved us. Do this and our prayers for each other shall be answered, — we shall have a happy New Year.

II.

THE MODEL CHURCH.

And fear came upon every soul, and many wonders and signs were done by the Apostles. And all that believed were together and had all things common; and they sold their possessions and goods, and parted them to all according as any man had need. And day by day, continuing steadfastly with one accord in the temple, and breaking bread at home, they did take their food with gladness and singleness of heart, praising God and having favor with all the people. And the Lord added to them day by day those that were being saved. — Acts ii. 43-47. (R. V.)

This is a description of the first Christian Church. Its officers had been chosen and trained by Jesus Christ. Its members, we are told, continued steadfast in the Apostles' teaching. Their fellowship was undisturbed by dissensions. They had favor with all the people — even "working men," that must include. Every day God added to them those who were being saved.

This is the only Church minutely described in the New Testament. It would therefore appear to be held before us as the ideal which other churches should try to realize and reproduce.

I. I would have you observe that it had an extremely simple creed, — personal loyalty to the Lord Jesus Christ. That and that alone qualified a man for membership. It was bound together, not by a consensus of intellectual opinions as political parties are, but, as families are, by affectionate obedience to a person.

II. The description of this Church forms the beginning of the Book of Acts. The biographies of the Apostles are not records of emotions, like the biographies of À Kempis and Tauler; nor of speculative controversies, as the history of the Church became after she had, at Constantinople, laid aside the crown of thorns for the diadem of pearls: but a book of acts.

It is said that one of the early hermits spent seventeen years standing in the attitude of prayer, until his knees had grown so stiff that he could not stoop to give drink to a sick man dying at his feet. The marvel is, not that such a story could gain credence, but that the hermit should pass for a saint among the disciples of Him who warned us not to make long prayers, and told us to imitate the good Samaritan. A church may come out of the Lenten season or the week of prayer like the stiff-kneed hermit. Whether, during appointed seasons of devotion, we really pray, the deeds which follow those seasons will inexorably indicate. The narrative of the days in the Upper Chamber, and of the Pentecost which followed them, would have described the Waterloo of Christianity, if it did not begin the Book of Acts. By this approach let us scrutinize the Model Church.

1. We are told that fear came upon every soul, that is, upon every member of the Church. So it seemed to Luke. Caiaphas, or Josephus, even Gamaliel, or any other than an inspired seer, would have written, " Fear departed from every soul." The most the Sanhedrim could discern was that certain timid men had grown bold and made others bold. A Galilean had been executed upon the double charge of blasphemy and sedition. His disciples had fled and sought concealment. For more than a month they kept in hiding. Then suddenly they reappeared. The hares had become lions. They met openly. They chose the most conspicuous places and occasions to publish them-

selves followers of their dead leader. They proclaimed that leader, whom the Jews had condemned for blasphemy and the Romans crucified for treason, the rightful King of both. They declared that the supreme crime possible to men was the denial of his authority. They entered the temple, which was the throne of Jewish sovereignty, where also a Roman garrison was quartered, and there, among civic rulers, exasperated churchmen, and Roman soldiers, they talked treason in the name of their lost leader with a reckless daring never paralleled by any body of men before or since. They rang in the ears of Jewish priest and Roman soldier, "This Jesus whom ye have crucified is both Lord and Christ." Luke describes this splendid bravery by saying, "Fear came upon every soul" which caught the fine contagion.

Luke was a seer. He described, not the obvious flower, but the hidden root. These men were fearless, he explains, because they feared God. That was the root of all their brave and beautiful deeds. This Church at Jerusalem had come to see Him who is invisible, and to realize that He was not on the side of Caiaphas, but of Christ. That conviction was the foundation of their character, the blood of their bravery. As Paul afterwards told the Corinthians to do, they went forward "perfecting holiness in the fear of the Lord."

The preacher often asks, "Whom do you love?" He does well to ask the question. But the Bible often asks, "Whom do you fear?" "For the fear of the Lord is the beginning of wisdom, and the knowledge of the holy, that is understanding." The man who fears God can be afraid of no other person; can fear no thing; neither life, nor death, nor principalities, nor powers, nor things present, nor things to come."

Something more than such valor is requisite to Christian manhood, to church prosperity; something greater than this, as the oak is greater than the acorn. John Baptist is less than the least in the kingdom of heaven. But without the fear of the Lord, even virtues are but artificial flowers glued upon the tree of life, not leaves for the healing of the nations. For where the fear of the Lord is not, the fear of men will be, and better Cromwell with his thunder than the gentlest singer singing soft songs because he is afraid to thunder. Better the Levite passing by on the other side than a Samaritan pouring in oil and wine because he fears the anger of the Jews if he neglects their countryman.

I think the Church in our time has need of exhortation to fear God. She is afraid of many things because she does not realize the awfulness of disobeying Him.

2. We are told that many signs and wonders were done by the Apostles. That Luke records the fact, without pausing to relate what the signs and wonders were, is a proof of inspired wisdom. Another historian would — as so many early Christian writers did — have lingered over the miracles. But Luke does not. He knew that miracles were not essential to church life. He wrote, not to appease curiosity, but to inspire conduct. Therefore he simply notes the fact that miracles were wrought, and passes on to record what is essential to church life. It is as if he had said, "The Apostles wrought miracles, but since you are not apostles the fact does not greatly concern you. But you are believers, and therefore need to know what all the believers did, and what you must do."

If we could pray sick men into health or

dead men back to life, most of us would think that supremely notable, and the newspapers would be filled with descriptions of the signs and wonders we could work. But in describing the Model Church, in which such miracles actually were performed, Luke diverts attention from them as if he held them immaterial; saying, "The Apostles wrought miracles, but all the members of the church did these other things."

3. Upon the next statement the inspired writer dwells with careful minuteness, as if he considered it supremely important. The members of this Church, he tells us, had that self-denying affection for each other, without which even their bravery would have been a king without a sceptre, a Gibraltar with no human garrison upon its breast of stone, a skeleton to inspire terror rather than a beautiful body of Christ to win love.

"All that believed were together, and had all things common; and they sold their possessions and goods and parted them to all, according as any man had need."

Well did such a miracle of love deserve the minute description it received, for it was the most perfect realization of heavenly society which has yet appeared among men.

Here, you will observe, is nearly the political economy of a Christian family. All things common; each receiving what he needs; the wisest and best deciding, with help of all, what each does actually require.

Here the Christian ideal was realized as it never has been since, and as it cannot be realized again, until men are once more brought under equally perfect control of the Spirit of God. These Christians were able to do what no other body of men have been able to achieve. Other attempts have been made to live in community of property, but they have miserably failed. The Apostles never advised it. Except this once, the apostolic churches never attempted it. But this Church practised it, and so long as the members retained the spirit in which they began, they were blessed. No equally convincing proof, I think, has ever been given by any other body of men that they were the visible body of Christ, filled with the Spirit of God.

"All that believed were together." Could you select a hundred men and women anywhere on earth who should be able to live in the same house, to meet not only once or twice a week, but every day, breaking bread together continually, surrounded by most bewildering and threatening circumstances, each driven by intense convictions, excited by most fervid emotions, and have never a jar? Many a church cannot have a fair without a quarrel.

And these Christians had not been trained, as we have been, under influences which tended to produce in them all the same tastes, the same habits. They had come from every nation under heaven. Some were rich, some were poor. Yet they had all things in common. If only the umbrellas in a modern church were held in common, on the first rainy day there would be trouble. But these Christians held houses and lands and all things so. One accustomed to luxury resigns his wealth without repining. Another trained in want gives up his poverty without becoming arrogant. Each receives, not what he craves, but what he needs. If that were tried to-day, what murmurings, what snatchings, would result! Let Fourierism, let Brook Farm, let the Knights of Labor, reply! Coleridge, I count the most commanding intellect, and Southey one of the most perfect characters, this century has seen. They are starting to establish upon the banks of the Susquehanna their ideal society. All property is to be held in common, and peace and brotherhood to be perfected in love. But they can get no farther than Bristol without striking upon a pocket difficulty which shatters their golden ship!

Born brothers cannot so live when they have passed that period of childhood which represents the kingdom of God on earth. The delirium of anarchy always follows when community of property precedes. In time the system proved too heavenly for even this noble Church to maintain. They could not long live on angels' food. Others less spiritually-minded joined them. Perhaps the original members grew lax. Then began certain Hellenists to complain that their widows were neglected in the daily ministrations. But a considerable time elapsed before murmurs disturbed their peace. They rejoiced together and praised God continually. No one received more than it was best for him to have. Each must have loved his neighbor as himself. Each must have been too zealous about laying up treasures in heaven to mind about laying up treasures on earth. The entire Church must have been as you have seen a family where sickness has lifted its sweet sceptre and the charity of heaven fills the house. Each walks softly; is eager to watch or to run, thinking not of his own things but of the things of the sick one, as God thinks of the one sheep. Then for a little while the wings of death shed the glory of God on earth, as if the Father had told him to comfort those that mourn, by giving them some right conception of the heaven to which he for whom they mourn has been taken.

This early Church actually realized for a season that ideal state which has been the dream of humanity in all ages; which has been the aim of all socialists whose failures are the blotches of history. This early Church realized in fact a social condition which George MacDonald has ventured to describe only as an insane man's dream of heaven.

Would I have you attempt such an arrangement here? Would I have you attempt to kindle a fire with blocks of ice! Community of property would instantly draw into your membership those who will not dig and are not ashamed to beg. But that it would not do if joining the church meant risking your life. Persecution was the careful guardian of the Church at Jerusalem. From us that guardian has been withdrawn.

When the right fuel is on the hearth of Christ the fire will easily be kindled. Till then this picture in the text must stand before us as a revelation of the greatness of the change we need to fit us for the kingdom of heaven. Trying to do what the first Church did would be trying to pull rosebuds into roses with dental forceps. Trying to be what the first Church was will water the roots, and make the roses in due time appear.

4. "They continued steadfastly with one accord in the temple." Observe the fidelity of these men to their trust. The temple was God's house. They were God's servants, God's children. At the risk of their lives they continued to claim their rights and perform their duty by worshipping in their Father's house.

These early Christians were related to the temple much as we are related to what men call the world. By "the world" to-day is meant, not what the Apostles meant by the same expression, but the broad life of humanity, the business, the pleasure, the arts, the sciences, the industries of men. All these are Christ's. It is the business of the Church to claim them in his name. When false men, when wicked men, usurp control of them, the Church is cowardly and recreant to her Lord if she leaves such men in undisputed control of her Lord's possessions. The earth is the Lord's and—not the emptiness thereof, as some appear to think—but the fulness thereof. To the last moment, when the temple itself was destroyed, the followers of Christ claimed it for their Father and his Son. There Stephen stood; thither Peter and John went daily; there, when Stephen had been stoned and Peter imprisoned, Paul asserted his right to be; thither he returned, when he had been cast out, again and again, and from the temple at last James the Just was hurled.

Though their dearest, tenderest devotion was not here, but in the inner circle of believers; though they met privately, not because they feared to meet openly, but because it was sweeter to break bread together with Christ alone, yet did these brave, kind men claim their rights in the temple their Father had given them in the world which was God's. But what pleasant thing, what profitable thing, what thing which men love, whether in business, art, science, recreation, can be named which some coward Christians have not renounced as the property of Satan!

5. "Praising God." These members of the Model Church were glad men, singing men. The times were sick. The world had never been so sad as in their day. There was enormous wealth. There were innumerable appliances for pleasure. But men no longer enjoyed their books, their pictures, their games, their banquets. Dives' heart was heavy. Faring sumptuously every day, clothed in purple and fine linen, the Roman noble kept his bath of perfumed water warm, that he might lie down in it, open an artery, and pass without pain into what he hoped would be oblivion, if some small grain of peril or despondency should be added to the burden beneath which he continually labored and was heavy-laden. Those who were not enormously and iniquitously rich were extravagantly poor; not in honorable, sturdy

poverty, but in servile beggarly poverty, that festered and fawned and chose to flatter rather than to starve. The consciousness of God and immortality had vanished from the Roman world. That world had become a fetid chamber, in which charcoal braziers glowed. Poisoned by the fumes and by their own breaths, men looked hopelessly into each other's ghastly faces and knew not what ailed them. They only knew that pleasures no longer pleased.

The first Church was a ventilator opened by Christ. The air of heaven rushed in, bringing life and joy to smothering humanity. More than any other of its features, the joyousness of Christianity first attracted and fascinated mankind. The soldiers came asking what it was that made men sing while they were butchered, though the butchers could never sing. And is not the world sad to-day? Is it not faring sumptuously with a sickly appetite? And whence should spring the fountain of joy if not from the Church of Christ? Who should be wells of water springing up unto eternal life?

Would that the world might see in us a flock led beside still waters, in green pastures — a company of men and women begirt with all the common ills of life, bearing all the burdens that weigh down other men, but minding those burdens no more than travellers mind the dust and cinders that fall upon them in the railroad train that carries them home! Then would the world observe, wonder, and wish to come among us.

"Joy to the world, the Lord is come." To say that to men in some convincing way is the business of the Church.

6. "Having favor with all the people." The true way to win men is shown us here. For a little while we may win popularity by pandering for it. But they who win and keep the favor of their fellows are they to whom man is little and God is all. Therefore we read the great distinction of the Model Church in this: "The Lord added daily to it those who were being saved."

To such a church men must be drawn as iron filings to a magnet; a church where the fear of the Lord makes the members brave, so brave that they can be always kind, can wholly love not only one another, but even the enemies that stone and kill them; a church filled with men always glad because the springs of their joy are high in the hills where drouth never comes. Brave, loving, faithful, glad men and women, the Church at Jerusalem was indeed the visible body of Christ. Therefore men sought to touch it, and as many as touched were made whole.

III.

TEACH US TO PRAY.

> And when ye pray, ye shall not be as the hypocrites; for they love to stand and pray in the synagogue and in the corners of the streets, that they may be seen of men. Verily I say unto you they have received their reward. But thou, when thou prayest, enter into thine inner chamber, and having shut thy door, pray to thy Father which is in secret, and thy Father which seeth in secret shall recompense thee. And in praying use not vain repetitions as the Gentiles do, for they think that they shall be heard for their much speaking. — MATT. vi. 5-7. (R. V.)

It is the beginning of the week of prayer. In place of the programme offered by the Evangelical Alliance, we have assigned for the subject of each day one of the seven petitions in our Lord's Prayer. Selections of Scripture calculated either to explain the meaning or hold the mind to contemplation of the subject of each petition are named upon the cards handed you this morning. By keeping our thoughts resolutely for an entire day upon each of these objects of desire it is hoped that we shall learn to obey in some measure the command: "After this manner therefore pray ye."

But the dangers against which the Master bids us guard ourselves, whenever we try to pray, become especially formidable at a time like this. I will try to open your eyes to them this morning.

I. It would be difficult, I think impossible, to prove that our Lord ever commanded his disciples to pray. "Watch and pray, lest ye enter into temptation," is shown by the context to be the granting of a privilege rather than the enforcement of a duty. Jesus always assumes that his disciples pray; teaches them plainly that unless they pray they cannot do what they must do. A man cannot work unless he eats. The harder he works the more imperatively he will realize his need of food. But there are no commandments in any code declaring that men shall eat. If they have no appetite they cannot; if they have, they do not need to be commanded.

But nothing is more common with religious teachers than to tell men it is their duty to pray, as it is their duty to tell the truth. Thus men have been led to assume that they can pray by resolving to do so, and the result is, so little real prayer that perhaps a majority are able to doubt whether praying is not folly, and to feel the need of prayer-tests to prove that our Father in heaven is to be thought of in the figure of parental considerateness rather than under the form of parental obstinacy or deafness.

Our Lord moved his disciples to pray, not by telling them to do so, but by exciting in them desires which compelled them to supplication. When they saw Him with Moses and Elias, they began to pray; when they watched Him healing diseases, they began to pray; when they heard Him praying, they straightway asked Him to teach them how to pray.

If you are dying through inability to eat, you cannot cure yourself by simply resolving to swallow food. You must take measures to restore your appetite. Neither can you pray by direct force of resolution. You must put yourself under conditions which will inspire desire for communion with God.

1. Because for most men it is hard to pray, and easy to pretend, we are warned against that easily besetting sin.

" When ye pray, be not as the hypocrites are."

The hypocrites wanted of the king only to be seen in his company. They stood at his door that they might be mistaken for his friends.

The same temptation assails us at all times, and is acutely dangerous now. It is insidious as malaria. It saps the health of piety before its presence is suspected; has depraved many an honorable pagan into a sanctimonious Pharisee; and we will be wise to remember what Mr. Ruskin has said with truth, that "the rottenest thing about a rogue is always his religion."

2. Most of us say grace before our meals. If we realize who feeds us, we cannot help doing so unless we are brutes. Most of us have family worship. If we are alert to spiritual facts, it will be more natural to omit our meals than our devotions.

But what are the motives we often hear unblushingly advanced for continuing these spiritual exercises? The children will be surprised if they do not hear grace at table! For the sake of the example upon them, daily prayers must be inexorably maintained.

But is it permitted to pray that we may be seen of children, and forbidden to pray that we may be seen of men? Coleridge says he "once knew a small but (in outward circumstances at least) respectable congregation, four fifths of whom professed that they went to church entirely for the example's sake; in other words, to cheat each other and act a common lie." When the minister leads in prayer, you all assume the attitude of worship. Not to do so would appear ill-bred. Those of you who arrive during prayer-time stand silently in reverential attitudes near the door. While you stand or sit with closed eyes and bowed heads, are you really communing with God? Are you thinking of Him? Is your spirit actually employed as your body advertises it to be? If not, why do you assume the attitude of worship? I can conceive no other motive — though probably no one is aware of it — than the desire to be seen of men. I suppose that is what the dread of appearing ill-bred means. Christ forbids us to assume attitudes in order that we may appear unto men to pray, especially when we are not praying. What would be the impression created if, while we bowed together in praying postures, one should take out a letter and begin to read it; another should speak of a sleighing party; another begin to cipher upon the hymn-book last week's profits, or the chances of next week's election; and another inquire how soon the minister would be through? No one would be satisfied to have the prayer continue in the midst of such a Babel. All would summon the minister to stop.

But does He who looks not at the outside of us never witness a similar confusion? If so, is it strange that what we call our "united prayers" have no conspicuous results?

3. This week every professing Christian who does not pray will be powerfully tempted to pretend he does. The world expects you to pray. Your brethren expect you to pray. You expect yourself to pray. Devotional meetings are multiplied. They are arranged for every day, and several times a day. If you attend none of them, with your training and views of duty, you cannot help feeling in some degree as a soldier feels when he shirks his duty. You will therefore be tempted to come to the meetings and assume the appearance of devotion, in order to be seen of those men of whom you yourself are one.

But how can this temptation to pious pretence be mastered?

Christ tells us in the text. The closet is the cure for hypocrisy in prayer. There is no recorded prayer from our Master's lips which could have occupied three minutes in its utterance, but we know He often spent whole nights in solitary communion with God. No man goes into his closet to be seen of men, for there men cannot see him. The more we have to pray in public, the more we must pray in secret, if we preserve the integrity of our spiritual manhood.

For this reason the cards inviting you to the meetings this week ask you to come through your closets. It will be hardly possible for any one to read and ponder the Scriptures selected and marked for each day, without receiving such impressions of God's presence and power and love as will make men seem small and their opinions trivial. If any one is obliged to choose between coming to the meetings, and carefully pondering the readings at home, it will be better for him to observe the readings at home, even if he has to omit the meetings. Twenty of us coming together at the close of a day spent in breathing the spiritual atmosphere of Moses and Elias, of Paul and John; at the close of a day in which we have walked in imagination each alone from Sinai to Calvary, or among the kings, the beggars, and the peasants of Palestine in the company of Jesus, will be able to pray together free from all thought of being seen by men.

II. When we pray, we are forbidden to use vain repetitions as the heathen do. The Jews had borrowed from Egypt and from Babylon the superstition here rebuked. They believed there was magical power in certain combinations of words. If repeated a certain number of times, even by one who did not understand their meaning, it was held that sickness would be cured and demons cast out. The foolish notion in later times ripened into the system of the Cabala, which assumed that mysterious efficacy inhered in a certain arrangement of mere letters. No one of us supposes himself infected by that folly. Yet most of us are.

There are men, good men, men meaning to be honest, who think their prayers must be right if they are couched in Scriptural phrases. Many say prayers every night and every morning, who never pray except when they are scared.

Repeating David's or Isaiah's petitions, or even our Lord's Prayer, is not necessarily praying because we do it on our knees. Saying over even the Lord's Prayer is for us a vain repetition until we so understand its meaning and so sympathize with its spirit that the words express our real desires. For "vain repetitions" are simply "empty phrases," sayings which do not express what we really mean.

1. Most of us dread a spot of silence in the prayer meeting. "Let no time be wasted," from the lips of the leader, implies and expresses the general conviction that, even when we have nothing to say, it is better to say it, because we are praying to be seen of men.

2. One rises to pray. His spiritual development has reached just far enough to make him realize God's goodness and desire God's care. But only in a vague and general way. He begins: "We thank Thee, O God, for thy goodness. We pray Thee to take care of us." This much is genuine prayer. But he feels it will not do to stop yet. He must keep on two or three or five minutes at least. He catches Scripture phrases, or familiar sentences which other men have genuinely and sincerely spoken. The first twenty seconds was prayer, the rest vain repetition. Many

a man can pray half a minute, when to pray a minute requires more spiritual-mindedness than he possesses.

With no man is the danger of making vain repetitions so great and so constant as with the minister. He cannot pray in the great congregation unless he has brought himself by much meditation to realize the needs not only of himself, but those of other men, and made them in some degree his own burden.

3. There are certain things we know we ought to desire. We feel guilty if we realize that we do not. But if we ask for them when we do not want them, we are making vain repetitions.

Yet how many pray volubly for Foreign Missions who never give a dollar for God to employ in answering their petitions! How many pray for the divine blessing upon their country who do not care enough for its welfare to vote!

The cure for this habit of making vain repetition lies in creating right desires. We must learn to know what we need, and to desire that. Therefore we are told, —

III. When we pray, to pray after this manner.

After warning us against praying to be seen of men, and against vain repetitions, the Master gives positive directions.

That the words were not material is evident because the three evangelists do not report the same words. The Lord's meaning must be, "When ye pray, pray in this spirit, with these desires." The prayer tells us what we need, but rarely crave. If we were sure that one wish, and one only, would be granted us this day for the asking, would that wish be the petition which stands first in the Lord's Prayer? Does not the whole tenor of our lives imply that, if we were entirely honest with ourselves, the most imperative desire of this man is to be rich, of that man to be praised, of the third man to have the life of his child spared? You will find the prayers in the New Testament ask for none of these things except in a very subordinate way. It is not forbidden to desire them. It is not forbidden to ask for them. It is forbidden to desire them first, to ask for them first, to labor for them first, and that most of us do. Three facts appear distinct as sunlight: —

1. That we shall not pray effectively until we pray according to the mind of God.

2. That few of us do greatly desire the things God desires for us.

3. That we need such a change of heart as shall make us crave what God declares we need.

And this is only another way of saying, —

1. That we cannot pray effectually until we can sincerely pray in the manner of our Lord's Prayer.

2. That few of us can yet do that.

3. That we need to learn to do so.

For this reason you are asked to spend this week in honest contemplation of that prayer.

My friend and brother! Suppose no mortal were present. Suppose yourself assured that your dearest wish would be realized. I will suppose you to have been rich. But now you are poor. You are struggling against inevitable bankruptcy. To-morrow the secret will be out. In the black future you see attachments; you see your long-honored credit gone, your good name dragged in the dirt, your wife and children in want. Now with perfect honesty say, is the first desire of your heart, is your dearest wish, this: "Our Father who art in heaven, hallowed be thy name"? If not, be sure it ought to be. I have only described the position upon which his disciples were entering when Jesus told them to pray "after this manner." We need to lay fast hold of those influences which will inspire such desires as can be faithfully expressed by the petitions the Lord would have us offer.

Widowed wife, the life of your only son hanging by a hair, is your first wish "Thy will be done"? Then have you not need to realize those facts revealed and impressed in the Scriptures which will make you turn to your Father's love as your son trusts yours, and desire that his will may be done, even though that means a sword through your heart?

But weak mortals cannot rise to such heights! We cannot feel thus! Paul felt so. He asked for what he wanted, not for what he knew he ought to want. When we are filled with desires like his, we shall receive blessings like his. When we can sincerely pray, "Thy kingdom come," be sure the kingdom will come.

IV.

THE KEYS OF THE KINGDOM.

And I also say unto thee, that thou art Peter, and upon this rock I will build my church; and the gates of Hades shall not prevail against it. I will give unto thee the keys of the kingdom of heaven; and whatsoever thou shalt bind on earth shall be bound in heaven, and whatsoever thou shalt loose on earth shall be loosed in heaven. — MATT. xvi. 18, 19. (R. V.)

THE essential difficulty of this passage and of the two others it brings to mind is this: Jesus told Simon that he should be called a Rock-man. He afterwards called him a Rock-man. Yet the narrative of the New Testament shows that of all the disciples Peter was least like a rock. He was the most impetuous, the most mobile, the least stable of them all. His age, for he appears to have been the oldest, his impetuosity, the ardor of his affection, and his powers of sympathy qualified him for leadership. But in steadfastness which is the characteristic of a rock, he was eminently deficient. It is never possible to understand our Master's meaning by blinking facts, even though our motives may be reverential. If we will give due weight to the obvious peculiarities of Peter's character, it will be evident that the words of the text were not intended to remind him of his strength, but to warn him of his weakness.

The context implies as much: " Blessed art thou, Simon Bar Jonah." Immediately, as if another fact needed to be kept in mind, our Lord adds, " I also say unto thee." Then follows the text.

It emphasized by repeating in three distinct illustrations the same fact. These are the pictures: —

1. A building — the Church — of which Peter is to be the foundation stone.

2. A city or a house in which Peter is to be the porter.

3. A wood-yard or a fountain where Peter is to bind the loads or the water-jars upon the carriers who bear them into the city. For observe it is not " whomsoever ye bind," but " whatsoever ye bind."

Thus Peter is reminded that he is to serve as the foundation of a building, the porter of a dwelling, a binder or unbinder of loads.

In each of these figures the emphasis belongs not, where it has been carelessly placed, upon the words "rock," "keys," "bind on earth," but upon those which express the importance of the work to be done. The common laws of Greek emphasis suggest if they do not compel the reading: "Thou art Peter, and upon this rock will I build my church, *and the gates of Hades shall not prevail against it*," *i. e.* the church which shall endure for ever; the point of the illustration being the permanence of the building.

"I will give unto thee the keys of *the kingdom of heaven.*" The attention is here drawn to the value of the trust.

"Whatsoever thou shalt bind on earth *shall be bound in heaven.*" The momentous nature of the issues at stake is emphasized.

Suppose yourself a master builder. You say to the masons, "I mean on these foundations to rear a structure that shall endure until the last trumpet sounds." Certainly you would be understood as warning the masons to exert their utmost care.

You serve in a great mansion. The mistress, intrusting you with keys, explains: "These are the keys, not of the ash-bin, but of the medicine-chest and the silver closet."

You are a physician. You see me binding a load upon the back of my child, and tell me it will curve his spine for life to carry that.

In each of these figures the same truth was pressed upon Peter. "Be faithful, be steadfast, for tremendous responsibilities are placed in your charge." This was the lesson Peter most needed to be taught. It was the lesson Christ in other ways and at other times urged upon him. It was the lesson which in a few moments, when the Master shall be compelled to rebuke his wilfulness, Peter will hear repeated in the stern utterance, "Get thee behind me, Satan."

I. It is apparent therefore why the words of the text were first and specially addressed to Peter. For Peter we know was, of the eleven, the most likely to forget his trust. He oftenest had occasion to repent. He oftenest needed forgiveness. For Peter Jesus showed the most solicitude. Peter He warned most earnestly. For Peter He prayed that his faith might not fail. It was Peter whose fidelity, faltering in time of trial, He strove to steady beforehand by reminding him of the magnitude of his trust. It was Peter whom, at the last supper, He prepared for the coming storm by putting him specially in charge of the rest.

If you were leaving the house in your children's care, you would warn them all to watch until you returned. But upon the one whom you knew to be most heedless you would strive most earnestly to impress the danger of playing with matches. To the one you thought most passionate and wayward you would say, "Remember, the credit of the family rests with you; see to it that, whatever the others do, you are kind and gentle." So Jesus, when He began to foretell his own departure, reminded Peter how much depended upon him, and said to him, "Strengthen thy brethren."

II. Neither of the three illustrations used by Christ was new to the disciples. They had heard Him denounce the priests at Jerusalem for precisely that misuse of divinely given opportunities against which He is now warning themselves. Those priests also had been divinely commissioned to be foundations in the kingdom of God, and porters to open unto men. They, too, had been appointed to unbind heavy burdens. But they had perverted their functions to the service of their pride, and, though they had been chosen to minister as children of heaven, the Master himself described them as the "children of hell."

The man who was at the moment the most prominent example of Jewish priestcraft — who stood before the world as the head of that godless, selfish, arrogant, ambitious, avaricious, unscrupulous, and cruel hierarchy for the reformation of which our Lord never expressed a hope, the high priest who declared it was expedient that Christ should die — was also named Rock-man.[1] That wicked and apostate priest was, not so much by his own individuality as by his representative position, the conspicuous example of all that a disciple ought not to be, — of all that Peter would become unless the impulses he had already shown, and would display still more clearly before the passing interview should end, were eradicated. Joseph Caiaphas was only Simon Peter refusing God's gracious guidance and full grown. "Get thee behind me, Satan!" was addressed to that infant tendency revealed in Peter which, grown to giant proportions in the Jewish hierarchy, called forth the supreme denunciations against those whom our Lord designated as children "of their father

---

[1] Cephas and Caiaphas appear to be the same word, though it is right to say that the great authority of Professor Thayer is against the identification.

the devil." To those whose ears were full of the awful woes uttered against the Pharisees, at a time when the most influential member of that religious sect which Christ would certainly destroy was named Rockman, there must have been a tremendous warning in the words addressed to the most influential member of the organization which Christ was about to establish, "Thou, too, shalt be called Rock-man, and upon this Rock will I build my church."

The second figure was equally familiar. For the disciples had heard their Master denounce the religious teachers of the time because they had taken away the key of knowledge intrusted to their care, and would neither enter in themselves nor suffer others to go in. In a few days they would hear their Master cry, "Woe unto you, scribes and Pharisees, hypocrites! For ye shut up the kingdom of heaven against men!" With such denunciations fresh in mind, Peter first and the disciples afterwards heard our Lord say, "I will give unto you the keys of the kingdom of heaven."

The third figure was equally familiar. How often had the twelve heard the Master say, as he raised the fallen, healed the sick, preached glad tidings to the poor, and opened the prison doors to the prisoners, "The scribes and Pharisees sit in Moses' seat; all therefore whatsoever they bid you observe, that observe and do; but do not ye after their works: for they say and do not. For they bind heavy burdens and grievous to be borne, and lay them on men's shoulders, but they themselves will not move them with one of their fingers." The disciples knew that their Master came to unbind burdens, and make men free for time and for eternity. They knew the leaders of the Jewish Church were under his unqualified denunciation because they had not done that, but had bound the burdens they were set to loose. And now they hear Him tell themselves that to them it is given to loose men, not for time alone, but for eternity. Woe will it be to them if, when they are sent to loose, they also bind.

How sorely Peter needed these warnings presently appears. For, the moment Jesus began to tell what He meant to suffer for the sake of opening the kingdom to men and unbinding their burdens, Peter's vanity, ambition, and selfishness, the Caiaphas traits in him, awoke. He begins to play pope instantly. He protests, and Christ answers in the sharpest rebuke ever administered to one of the disciples.

III. We see why these same warnings, first addressed to Peter, were repeated, as appears from the 18th chapter of Matthew, to all the disciples. If those eleven men had proved indolent or faithless, the kingdom of heaven would not have been opened unto us. For to them the keys were given; on them the Church was built; they have unbound the burdens which press men to perdition. They were not gods; they were not even angels. They were tempted, as their predecessors, the Jewish doctors, had been tempted, as all their successors in office have been tempted, to pride, to arrogance, to indolence, to cowardice.

IV. Thus the text shows us the Master, while laying the foundations of the Christian Church, warning the builders against that danger which has always been the most universal, the most persistent, and the most insidious the Church has had to meet. All ecclesiastical history bears constant testimony to the inveterate tendency in the men whom Christ sends into the world, as his Father sent Him into the world, to repeat the crimes of Caiaphas. To make Christianity a temporal kingdom rather than an eternal power; to take away from men the key of knowledge, and, when ignorance grows dense enough to make it possible, to rule by fostering superstition rather than by feeding faith, — these have been the arch crimes of the Church. The kingdom of God has advanced only by successive rebellions inspired by the Holy Spirit against the usurpations of those who were sent forth to minister among brethren, but who have insisted upon getting themselves called masters and lords, and using the towels given them to gird themselves for humble services in imitation of the Master, as banners to inscribe with emblems of pride and flaunt before the eyes of men.

The text says to every one of us who occupies in the Church a position of the least influence or authority, "The keys of the kingdom of heaven are in your hand; see to it how you employ them! Are you entering in yourself? Are you opening unto others?" Many are still carrying their keys as Peter for a time carried his. Until the enemies came, he followed Jesus, disputing, contradicting, disobeying. Headstrong in going his own way, he was continually getting himself rebuked. There was little peace in that for him. When danger came, he shirked. Then he mingled slyly with the Lord's enemies. Not much peace in that! The cock crew; he repented and wept bitterly. All the while he carried the key to the kingdom of peace unused. He would not forget himself, nor obey his Master humbly, faithfully. He would be pope. When he was content to let another gird him, and follow where he did not wish to go; to resign all papal authority and accept the fact that, if the Lord would have John tarry till He came, that was nought to him; when he was content to mind his own ways, and feed the sheep and the lambs without arrogating authority over them, — he entered into peace, and was able to open the door for himself, and to lead others unto the true Bishop and Shepherd of their souls.

The text asks us also whether we are loosing burdens or binding them upon men's shoulders. There are so many ways in which we may do either, and scarcely know what we are doing!

Here is a little child. It is such an one as Jesus took in his arms and said, " Of such is the kingdom of heaven." She flutters about the house an embodied joy. She sings to the ceiling. She shouts to her little red shoes. She claps her hands, she knows not why, from sheer excess of gladness. She kisses the cat. When little tears come into her eyes, they are like the dewdrops on the rose: the next zephyr dries the flower. The queen of happy, unburdened beings is a healthy little child!

That being of more than fairy brightness has become a haggard woman. Discontent has ploughed her brow and pinched her eyelids. Disappointment and envy reign in her eyes and curl her lip. She cannot dress as her pride desires. She cannot gain the position she craves. All her small arts and dissimulations have not won the admiration for which she pines. She has married and her husband is no hero. She has children whom she loves, but she is ashamed because she cannot dress them richly as the children of her neighbors. She must toil by day and watch by night. Life is a burden, and she is afraid to die. The fierce, unresigned, discontented spirit will not be changed by death. The grave cannot take off the burden she bears. She must carry it into eternity.

Who bound the burden on her? The mother that bore her, the father that trained her in maiden years. Neither taught her the true facts of life and peace. They did not surround her with an atmosphere of love for God and trust in Him. They never taught her to go, as Mary went, to One who casts out all devils, whether they be vanity, care, anxiety, or fear; to One who makes the vessel tossed by the storm to be "in a great calm." They taught her to take much thought for this world, saying, "What shall we eat, and what shall we drink, and wherewithal shall we be clothed?" Until she had been long under their charge, she cared for none of those things. She was in the kingdom.

But there are women who cannot be bound. They are crowned queens. When sickness desolates their homes, when the husband fails, money goes, drudgeries increase, through days of toil and nights of watching, they say, by eye, voice, gesture, "Be not afraid! Let not your heart be troubled." And when death comes, they smile in the eyes of their beloved one and say, "Do not be sad for me! It is not such a hard thing to die!"

You shall find, when you receive the confidences of such women and learn the secret of their lives, that they often think of their mothers; that, when they were little children, they were taught, how they cannot altogether tell, but they were taught to realize that the unseen world is more real than the visible, and that all the things which make men afraid are shadows cast by a sun which will never set. Their mothers taught them that, and they teach it to their children.

Such is the loosing which pastors and deacons are sent into the Church to accomplish, and the opposite of that is the binding of which pastors and deacons are warned with appalling distinctness to beware.

V.

SPIRITUAL PLOUGHING.

And another also said, Lord, I will follow thee; but let me first go bid them farewell, which are at home at my house. And Jesus said unto him, No man, having put his hand to the plough, and looking back, is fit [lit. "well placed," *i. e.* in the right attitude] for the kingdom of God.—LUKE IX. 61, 62.

LET us beware of drawing from these words the foolish inference that it is better not to plough than to plough poorly; better to stay behind than to glance behind. It is folly not to do the best we can because we cannot do better than we can. Some are waiting until they are perfect Christians before they will begin to be Christians at all. Pride, aping humility, makes them ashamed to creep, and therefore they never learn to walk.

But our Lord was not speaking to one in danger of making that mistake. He was showing a disciple how to do in the right way what the disciple was undertaking to do in a wrong way.

The man had decided to go with Jesus. He asked leave only to return home and bid farewell to his family. He might never see them again. His request seems innocent and amiable. Yet Jesus replied to him: "You are beginning in a wrong way. You are like a farmer trying to plough with his eyes behind him."

Like certain other utterances of our Lord, that of the beam and the mote, of the old and new bottles, for example, this one glows with a sweet and subtle humor. Those who have watched a ploughman at his work will appreciate the figure, for it would be easy to show that, though the appearance of an Oriental ploughing with young steers was radically different from that of an American ploughing with horses, the sight of either would produce with almost equal vividness the impression upon which the significance of the text depends.

Perhaps no other kind of labor demands a more intense concentration of muscle, mind, and will, towards a single purpose, than does ploughing. The ploughman must note every motion of his two draft-horses. If either lags, the other will jerk the share out of line. What each brute intends must be foreseen, and loitering steps prevented by voice or whip. The ploughman must observe each root and stone before him, and be ready by swift and dexterous twist to cut through the one or ease over the other. His eye must be upon the drawing beam, for, if it too abruptly leaves the level, the handles, wrenched from his grasp, may hurl him aside or strike him to the ground. He must watch the opening furrow, and find footing by instant shifts from glebe to glebe as the softened earth yields and crumbles beneath his weight, or he will be thrown. Alert to each of these requirements, he must, like the steersman of a vessel, steadily sight his bearings by some stationary object far in front, or his furrow will curve. All this he must do on the jump to economize momentum, or his horses may be stalled. It is an exhilarating sight to watch the skilful ploughman, rushing his furrow forward, springing from clod to clod, holding the handles firm with masterful grip, wrenching them this way and that with superlative force, shouting to his horses, while the sweat beads his face and his whole body seems one flashing eye, the muscles strained like watch-springs in obedience to his stimulated vision.

So the yachtsman steers the craft that moves with bellying sail amid the ships and buoys and reefs and shallows of the crowded harbor.

"Skipper, you almost grazed that reef! Look back! the wake line touches the surf!"

But the skipper does not look back. His business is, forgetting those things that are behind, to reach forth unto those things that are before. One glance backward may bring wreck or collision.

Add to the skipper's gaze, the straining muscles, the beaded brow, the energetic motion, and you have the ploughman ploughing as he should.

While such an one presents a glorious emblem of victorious achievement, a man trying to plough with his eyes behind him is an equally impressive picture of pitiable impotence. No longer master of the strength of wood and iron vivified by vast brute force, he has become its slave. Flung hither and thither by each of an hundred obstructions, he is dragged forward, bruised, bewildered, until the handles are wrenched from his grasp and he is dropped or dashed upon the ground. Far better, far nobler even that, than not to try at all! But how different the appearance of the ploughman doing his work aright!

This pitiable picture our Lord held, as if it had been a mirror, before the disciple who wished to leave him only long enough to say farewell to friends he might never see again.

Life is here figured as a field which God has set us to plough. Upon it three classes of men appear:

1. There are those who move without regard to their orders or their duty. Their purpose is to live as easily and pleasantly as possible. They mean to enjoy the present; to enjoy virtuously, if that may be, but to enjoy. What questions may be asked them by and by, they refuse to consider.

Of such the text says nothing.

2. There are others trying to plough with their eyes behind them. They have seized the plough in order to be drawn by it to heaven. But they have found life no summer sea over which they can be carried smoothly gliding. They have found it an unbroken prairie that must be ploughed as it is passed. They are continually tripped and thrown by unexpected obstacles. They do not find the joy they crave. When demands upon their energies increase, they are

disturbed. When tribulation or persecution ariseth because of the word " by and by they are offended." Thus they learn by sad experience that religion which is not wings is always chains.

3. But there are men who begin and continue the Christian life as the instructed ploughman runs his furrow.

Let us mark three points in the Master's illustration which give reply to certain questions often asked of Christians by the world, by their own hearts, by the Holy Spirit: —

1. Why does God's kingdom come so slowly? Why is the Church not stronger? Why are my prayers so cold, so few?

One could scarcely glance upon the ploughman at his work, remembering Christ's words the while, and ask these questions twice. The marvel would rather seem to be that the kingdom does increase.

Survey the field of Christian ploughmen. Some are absorbed in watching and in criticising other people's furrows. Some are gazing back upon their own, recalling past experiences, at times anxiously, which is bad; at times proudly, which is worse. How few are eagerly alert to the work they themselves are set to do! How few are even sure that they have furrows to plough!

2. The Lord's words bring an answer to another question of serious practical import.

It is said the Church is losing, if she has not already lost, her hold upon young men. It is said that while the feeble come to her for help, while children rest in her bosom contented until they begin to think, while the sick and the sad seek solace in her arms, the stalwart, the commanding, the masterful no longer show the old alacrity in responding to her call. I will not pause to debate the truth of the assertion. You know that it is often made. When thistle-down is in the air, there must be thistles in some man's farm, and therefore all farms are in danger.

A distinctive characteristic of Christ's work was the enthusiasm He created among young men. The noblest, the most enterprising, the strongest were the quickest to take fire from his touch. We read of no young man who opposed Him, of no old man who followed Him. Why is this not true now? We are told the young refuse to join Christ's Church, because in youth the passions are imperative, and, until pleasures have begun to pall, men are loath to sacrifice the seen to the unseen, the temporal to the eternal. But the statement is not true. It is accurately the reverse of true. The young have always been readiest to give themselves for ideals. It is when life is fullest and sweetest that men are quickest to renounce it on due occasion given. Who, when the guns began to thunder, rushed to Sumter and to Richmond? Who, when danger threatens, are expected to be first in the breach? Always and everywhere that class which to-day is deemed most loath to join the Church; the class which was most prompt to follow Jesus eighteen hundred years ago,—young men, young women, in the ardor and energy of life's spring. Why does Christ now appear less captivating to the strong and to the able?

Is not an answer found in this, that we no longer preach Him with the old heroic ring?

There are so many weak ones, so many sufferers in the world! The Master's words to them are so endlessly winning, that we have been moved to repeat those words out of all due proportion, while we neglect his more strenuous calls.

"Blessed are they that mourn, for they

shall be comforted." But many do not mourn. Has Christ no message for them?

"Come unto me, all ye that labor and are heavy laden, and I will give you rest." But multitudes are not heavy laden. To multitudes the idea of rest is repugnant, because they are not weary. They carry life as a hunter bears his gun through an unflushed preserve. Has Christ no words for them? Ay, verily! But how rarely are those words repeated!

The current conception of a Christian is taken more largely from "Pilgrim's Progress" than from the Bible. In the New Testament the Christian is painted, not as one flying from a doomed city, but as a stalwart farmer ploughing the old growths of the old world under, until visions of a new earth no less than of a new heaven fill his horizon. He appears digging, as men dig who have discovered gold. He is called a fisherman, and what that means I have learned not only from much communion with my trout-rod, but still more clearly from watching the deeds of obscure heroes who sail in winter from Gloucester and Cape Breton; "a warrior," which means to me Grant or Sheridan; "a wrestler," and the sight of two muscular giants clinched for thirteen minutes in the tense, unyielding strain of the Græco-Roman grip, till the bursting of a blood-vessel forces one of them to give way, may teach the interpretation of that word; "a runner" of races (read Morris's "Atalanta" for that); "a boxer" (remember the marble Damoxines for that); "a flasher of light" (let Minot's on dark nights be your lexicon for that); and, superlative synonym for ceaseless, immeasurable splendor, of generous and helpful energy, "a follower," that is, "an imitator," "of Jesus Christ." Could you find a series of illustrations less suggestive than these of an average modern prayer-meeting?

The portrait of a Christian painted by the Master, which hangs foremost in the gallery of the gospels, represents a man with eyes flashing, nerves quivering, muscles corded, brow beaded, blood dancing, intellect quickened, heart bounding: "I am come that they might have life, and that they might have it more abundantly."

Is a woman trembling among the Pharisees, show her Christ standing beside her as Great Heart caring for Christiana and her children. Is Mary mourning for her brother, tell her that Jesus wept. But is a young man in the unslipped leash of life quivering with exultant expectation, make him see in Christ the Master of the chase.

The Christian has come to be thought of as one who endures rather than as one who does; as dead to this world rather than as alive to the eternal; as one who renounces toys rather than as one who takes victoriously treasures; as one ceasing to serve Satan rather than as one beginning to serve God. In our thought, we define him chiefly by negatives. He does not lie, nor steal, nor envy, nor bear false witness, nor rebel overmuch against God's providence. Until we break through some of these negations we rarely question our right to wear the uniform of Him who rides forth conquering and to conquer.

But the strong and the ardent hate negatives. If I say of the sun, "It is not red, nor blue, nor green, nor square, nor near," all that I say is true, and only the more false for being true. Say rather, "The sun is all colors transfigured into dazzling radiance, piercing everywhere, and quickening all things that have life." It is what a man is and does, never what he is not and does not, that truthfully describes him. But we have unconsciously come to define the Christian — not articulately, but in our thoughts — as one " who never does to others what he would not have others do to him." You have sung it in popular hymns, you have read it in Sunday-school books, you have heard it in the nursery when Charlie pinched Jamie. " How would you like to be treated so? You must never do to others what you would not have them do to you." That is no definition of a Christian. It is the definition of an oyster. Let us get it right in our inmost thought: " All things whatsoever ye would that men should do to you, do ye even so to them." That will send us into life-boats to rescue drowning women when other men are afraid to go; up ladders into burning houses, and into cities plagued with yellow fever, when other men are afraid to go! That will send us into hospitals singing cheerful songs when our own hearts are sad; will make us stand for the weak against the strong; for the truth when lies are popular. That will make us kind to those who revile us, honest to those who cheat us. That will make us treat our fiercest afflictions as the fine furnace treats the coal which it receives black and heavy into its own heart, but sends forth to others transmuted into warmth and light. That will set those who waste life whining over their troubles to singing of their mercies, and will convert all pharisees and hypocrites into loyal men and true. For it will force us to realize that whatever creeds may say, whatever experiences in the past, hopes for the future, or emotions in the present may have seduced us to believe, the Master has given us no warrant to call ourselves Christians, or to hope that we are building upon the rock, unless we have begun to " do these sayings of mine."

3. One other question presses upon many who read the text.

" Let me first go bid them farewell which are at home, at my house." Was the Master's reply intended to rebuke the disciple for loving his family, — to teach him not to care for wife and child?

Altogether the reverse, I think. The man assumed that to follow Christ was to forsake his family. It was the fatal blunder made by most Christians some centuries later, when they conceived that to run away from their duties, and try to save their souls by hiding in caves or monasteries, without a thought of the world their Master came to deliver, was the proper way to obey Him. To grant the man's request would have confirmed him in his error. It was needful to teach him that he could effectually care for wife and child only by following with unswerving gaze and unfaltering foot the Lord who gave them to him. No man ever obeyed Christ in singleness of heart without discovering that fact. This disciple, if he obeyed, learned it in due time, and learned it effectually, though when or how he learned it we are not told.

Here is wisdom: to look upon wife and children remembering not that Jesus Christ has given them to you, — which is the fruitful parent of strikes and lockouts, and divorces and anarchies of every kind, — but that God has given you to them; to look upon your country remembering that Jesus Christ has given yourself and your family to it; to consider all nations, and realize that Jesus Christ has given you, your family, your country, to the world which He came to reconcile to God. Follow Christ thus, and as far as in you lies you shall save all. Reverse this order, place Christ last, or second, and as far as in you lies you shall lose all.

There are still those who fancy, "If I follow Him I must say farewell to my dear ones, for they will not come with me." The text is only one of many proofs which teach us that not to follow Christ is to say to our dear ones, "Farewell forever."

VI.

JERICHO.

They took the city. — JOSHUA vi. 20.

THE children of Israel had crossed the Jordan. Forty years they had wandered in " that great and terrible wilderness." With hunger and thirst they were familiar. At last their eyes, long scorched with the glare of burning sands, are cooled by the sight of streams and grass. In place of arid plains, dreary gulches, angry crags, they see a rich, a tropical fertility. Fields of grain carpet the lowland; palm groves offer delicious shade; vineyards and olive orchards have come to view. The sterile waste is behind; the land that flows with milk and honey is before them. Their eyes behold its beauty; their feet press its margin.

Athwart the alluring garden rises a barrier strong and grim. Directly in their path stands Jericho, the military key to Palestine. Jericho must be captured, or the forty years of journeying through deserts will prove futile.

The obstacle may well have seemed insuperable. It was a walled city, probably the strongest in Southern Syria. In the time of Joshua, the science of military defence was better understood than the science of attack. Cities could build walls which assailants could not breach. Even ten centuries later a properly constructed fortress was impregnable to any artillery invented. Before Moses left Egypt the Cyclopean walls described by Dr. Schliemann had been raised at Tyrens and Mycene. The walled cities of Palestine, though not like them of stone but of brick, were imposing structures. The sight of them inspired such terror in the spies sent forth by Moses, that they fled back to their countrymen declaring the conquest of the land impossible, for they had seen cities "walled and very great." These walls of solid masonry, probably from thirty to seventy feet in thickness, and so high that the spaces they enclosed were described as "fenced up to heaven," defied direct assault.

Of the many fortresses in Palestine, Jericho appears to have been the most nearly impregnable. The Israelites had no siege engines; neither battering-ram, nor catapult, nor moving tower. Their only weapons were slings, arrows, spears. Against the walls of Jericho these were as straws and thistle-down.

There were two other passes by which Joshua might have entered the Promised Land. Neither of them was guarded. It is significant that God conducted him across the Jordan at the point where the strongest fortification in the country stood directly in his way; the point where the sole alternatives before him were victory that seemed impossible, or defeat that would be ruin.

Once before the Israelites had entered Palestine. Then they approached from the south, crossed the border unopposed, and fled back before they were attacked. But in conquering Jericho they virtually subdued the Promised Land.

I. No good or permanently pleasant possession is ever gained in this world except by overcoming obstacles. Jericho always bars the entrance to the Promised Land. We see some object of desire. We see the difficulties in the way. We wish they were removed. We attack them, if we dare, for the sake of what we see behind them. But in conquering our Jericho we always win something more precious than we see or seek. Is it wealth one longs for? It must be earned by toil, frugality, self-denial. Indolence must be overcome. Unless these difficulties have been mastered, wealth is no blessing. There are no beatitudes save such as are approached by steep and narrow ways.

Self-control, self-respect, — for these we must fight! A man has yielded to the bad sceptre of his passions. He wishes those passions were less strong. He forgets that only Bucephalus controlled can carry Alexander. He would escape temptation, and so elude transgression and subsequent remorse. True, the only peace possible to passionate men is the peace won by self-conquest, but "greater is he that ruleth his own spirit than he that taketh a city."

If only a man's purpose is right, every obstacle which keeps him from attaining it is there by God's own appointment. It is there for him to conquer. By God's grace he can conquer it, and by the victory he will gain more than he has asked or thought.

II. Consider the preparations. Two conditions were essential. The people must be prepared for victory. The obstacle must be removed.

1. For seven days the Israelites were kept marching around Jericho. They had never seen a walled city. Not in Egypt, for only two of them had been there. Not in the desert, for it contained none. Day after day they were forced to gaze upon the stupendous structure. From every point of view they were compelled to scrutinize its strength. Time is needed for objects really great in nature or in art to exert their full effect upon the mind. Niagara grows as we gaze upon it. Conversation was forbidden. It might divert attention. In silence the soldiers contemplated the mighty walls. Every hour forces them to feel more keenly that their own strength is impotence. It is flesh against brick and mortar. That every man of them must have realized before the seven days had passed. Not only do the besiegers learn to appreciate their weakness, but they advertise it to their foes. When first the rumors of an impending invasion reached the city, it was filled with panic. But as the strangers marched round and round the walls, fear of them must have changed into

contempt. One can almost hear the jeers from Jericho. "Do these unarmed vagabonds expect to capture us by blowing horns?" For, while the invaders marched in silence, ever and anon their priests blew upon trumpets quick, short, triumphant notes, such as in later times were used, echoes from this experience at Jericho, to usher in the year of jubilee.

These notes seemed to say to the chosen people: "Take heart, our victory is sure!" The more the army become impressed with its own impotence, the more amazing must these tones have appeared. The soldiers' eyes reported, with constantly increasing emphasis, "Victory is impossible!" But their ears, catching the triumphant notes from the trumpets of the Levites, reported continually, "Victory is sure!"

My friends, have you never been subjected to a similar discipline? Have you never been brought to a wall great and high with no implement with which to pull it down? Have you never been beset with difficulties which seemed to increase as you faced them? You walk around your Jericho. You see no place that can be breached; no open gate; no crevasse through which even one arrow can be shot. Hope begins to pass into despair. But listen. Open your ears to the notes that are blown for you by the trumpeters of God: —

"Behold, I will not fail thee nor forsake thee."

"They that are for thee are more than they which are against thee."

"When my father and my mother forsake me, then the Lord will take me up."

"No good thing will He withhold from them that walk uprightly."

"Let not your heart be troubled, neither let it be afraid."

"Fear not, little children."

"Heaven and earth shall pass away, but my words shall not pass away."

It is not when the victory is won that we need these promises. Blessed is the man who listens to the trumpets of jubilee while his eyes are fixed on the walls of Jericho.

2. Meantime God is not idle. The walls must be removed, or the city cannot be taken. Though no sign *appears*, they are being sapped. Slowly, inexorably, subterranean fires are kindling. Silently, through the seven days of preparation, the earthquake has been running mines beneath the

doomed city. Unconscious of their invisible antagonist, the men of Jericho look down upon their visible assailants with scorn and sneer. Conscious of their unseen Helper, the men of Israel look up at their visible foes and wait — watching. How they know not, when they know not, but that victory will be theirs they know. Theirs only to obey; theirs only to stand ready; theirs to believe and rest in the Rock that is higher than they, higher than the walls of Jericho. For they know they are obeying God.

My friends, it is always true that every obstacle which hinders goodness, every fortress which guards wickedness, is being undermined. Right rules. Wrong is doomed in this world. If you are on God's side; if your plan is right, your purpose pure, — your triumph is certain. Whatever hinders, whatever threatens, will go down. You may not see when or how. Wickedness often seems impregnable. But right is omnipotent. To-day Judas seems wise, Jesus unwise. But look again to-morrow. There is nothing so hard to believe, but there is nothing more true, than this: till the judgment of the prince of this world cometh, the prince of this world always seems stronger than the King of heaven. But the prince of this world is doomed. It is when men doubt this that the faith which saves fails them. Oh for the faith which, though it sees Christ fettered, convicted, crucified, and saying, "It is finished," still believes that, when the city which rejects Him is ploughed and sown with salt, its inhabitants nailed upon crosses over which carrion eagles gather, the crucified One shall stretch his sceptre from sea to sea, and lead the isles rejoicing in his law!

Be anxious about nothing but your duty. No Joshua, whom we may unquestioningly follow, stands before us. Whether we are doing God's work we must learn by other means. But learn we can, and if we are doing that, we shall be more than conquerors through Him that loveth us.

III. The victory.

I think the most marvellous fact in the narrative we are studying is not the boldness of Joshua in laying siege to such a city, nor the willingness of his army to begin it, nor the patient marching of the seven days, nor the amazing catastrophe which ensued, but the spirit in which the final assault was made.

You may fancy the invader's task was easy. When the walls were fallen, half the defenders perhaps crushed beneath the ruins, the remainder by terror incapacitated for resistance, was it not easy for the besiegers to march forward and slay the defenceless survivors? If you think so, I suspect you have not well considered the narrative. I know you have never experienced an earthquake. The marvel is that the invaders did not themselves fly, or stand petrified with terror until their opportunity was past.

Joshua's army was certainly less than two miles, probably less than a quarter of that distance, from Jericho. It lay in the edge of a palm-grove. Any shock sufficient to prostrate the massive walls of the city must have extended far beyond his camp. We must remember the necessary concomitants of a convulsion such as here occurred. They would have produced in a common army only panic and impotence.

The Israelites stood in battle line. At a divine intimation, they are ordered to raise the battle-cry. At that moment the solid earth beneath their feet begins to shudder, to quake, to heave in billows like the sea.

The tall palms sway like mainmasts. Some fall crashing to the ground. From the rocky defile on their right, crags and loosened boulders plunge with terrific noise upon the plain. Clouds of dust and sulphurous smoke obscure the sun. Electric discharges make the thickened air lurid, or thread the gloom with lines of fire. Thunderous detonations roar down the ravine that debouches from the west. The tumult grows fiercer. By the lightning's glare the walls that for seven days have stood like Gibraltar before their eyes are seen to tremble. Rents appear in the solid masonry. The rents gape into fissures. Through the rifts terrified men are visible. Suddenly, with the crash of avalanches, the walls vanish. They do not oscillate, they only disappear. Before the awful reverberations have ceased, the order, passed from trumpet to trumpet, rings along the line, " Charge ! " Then every man moved straight forward, over the heaving earth, over the debris of shattered rocks and crushed palms, through the dust and sulphur clouds. How do these soldiers know the earth may not open and ingulf them?

Let such experience occur to an ordinary army, it would help them not at all until hours had passed. Imagine what your emotions would have been. Would you not have felt that omnipotent power was working in wrath, or that the forces of nature were blindly destroying?

But the Hebrews felt it was their God working for them. The earthquake was his voice. Therefore it could not harm, it must help them. Forty years of training had taught them this. They believed in Him who had parted the Red Sea, and shown himself in pillars of fire and of cloud for their sakes.

Such is the faith Christians need to-day. There is gloom on the faces of many, even among God's people. Anxiety is in their hearts. And why? Because the walls of Jericho are rocking, the walls of Jericho are falling.

The civil, the industrial, the religious world on both sides of the sea is troubled as in our time it has not been before. At the beginning of last winter, a few owners of coal-mines in Pennsylvania decreed that every poor man on the continent should find it harder to keep warm than it ought to be. 700,000 working men, through their representatives at Richmond, encamped with strong entrenchments against that castle of Giant Despair. We have all been hit by the missiles flying between castle and besiegers. Newspapers with large circulations are openly advocating anarchy, murder, and pillage. There is not a man in the country who has not been in some way warned of the danger threatening from the conflicts of labor and capital. What the end shall be no one knows. But only the reckless and the frivolous are without concern. Herr Most, though himself a trifle light as thistle-down, by his want of weight serves well to show how the winds are setting.

In the religious world anxieties are many. Some fear that the faith delivered us by the Apostles is in danger. The splendid work once done by the American Board is suspended. While millions upon millions are stumbling and perishing in the darkness at home and abroad, those whom Christ has commissioned to give them light have ceased to hold up the lamp of life while they debate whether white light or blue light is the best.

Many good men feel the ground quaking.

But let us be full of faith. God is removing those things that are shaken, that the things which cannot be shaken may remain.

Now is the time to pray as we have never prayed! To labor as we have never labored! To give money as we have never given money for Jesus Christ! For God is multiplying opportunities for true Christian work. Men are weary of quibbles, though many religious teachers have not yet discovered the fact. Men are hungry for the true bread that cometh down from heaven. God has prepared the way for a revival of that true religion which consists in loving Him with all the heart, and one's neighbor as one's self.

This is the bugle-call to us, this single fact, — that never since the world began have men been so eager as they are to-day to know the simple words and works of Jesus Christ, and so prompt to recognize the obligation they are under to obey Him and follow in his steps.

VII.

GIDEON'S MEN.

And the Lord said unto Gideon, By the three hundred men that lapped will I save you and deliver the Midianites into thine hand. — JUDGES vii. 7.

THE Midianites had conquered Palestine. They had not settled in the land, for they were rovers. The desert was their ocean, camels their ships, Palestine their victualling and coaling station. Every year, when the harvests were ripe, they landed at the rich plain of Esdraelon, stripped the country of its produce, and, after rioting awhile, as pirates in port, swept off again upon their wide voyages over the boundless desert. They came in irresistible numbers. Their chiefs, clad in barbaric splendor, rode upon camels caparisoned with trappings of scarlet and chains of gold. At their approach the Israelites forsook the plain, abandoned their flocks and their harvests, and sought safety in the caves of the hills. Year after year had this shame and terror been repeated, when Gideon attempted to organize resistance.

The tents of Midian covered the plains of Jezreel when, we read, the Spirit of the Lord came upon Gideon, and he blew a trumpet and sent messengers throughout all Manasseh, Asher, Zebulon, and Naphthali, the tribes which bounded or lay nearest to the camp of the invaders. The first blast of the trumpet sorted the nation. The servile-spirited, the indolent, those who were content to endure lives of shame beneath oppression and to be dumb driven cattle, paid no heed to the trumpet. But all whose manhood had not yet been crushed, all in whom sparks of patriotism still glowed, all who were ready to risk one blow for freedom, rallied at the call. Their number was small. Only thirty-two thousand responded to the summons.

The Midianites — like grasshoppers for multitude — were encamped upon the plain of Esdraelon. That plain, the historic battle-ground of Palestine and the garden of Southern Syria, shrinks towards the east, before it reaches the Jordan, into a narrow valley. The south wall of this valley is the range of Gilboa. In the time of Gideon that range was heavily wooded, and upon its northern slope there appears to have been a water-course. The channel was probably dry during part of the year, for no perennial stream exists at the spot where the spring of Harod seems to be necessarily located by the narrative; and though it is not possible to dissent without hesitation from the views of Canon Tristram, neither is it possible to identify the well of Harod with the spring of Jezreel, which flows at the base of the hill, without confusing the description of the battle.

In the thick wood upon the north slope of Gilboa, beside the upper stream, Gideon's men assembled. Probably signs of panic appeared among them when they perceived the numbers and strength of their foes. Guns in sight are more impressive than guns beyond the horizon. But cowards will be only an encumbrance here, and that Gideon knows. Therefore he issues orders for every one who is faint-hearted and every one who is afraid to return home before the descent from the hill is made. Twenty-two thousand departed. This fact, I suppose, and not the subsequent panic of the Midianites, gave the stream the name it bears in the narrative, "The Spring of Harod," or "Cowards' Creek."

The ten thousand who remained were all brave men. But more than courage was required in a battle such as Gideon had to fight.

There had been two sortings already, — one by the trumpet, another at "Cowards' Creek." A third was needed. There is no lesson we need to lay more to heart than this: in every strenuous campaign quality counts for more than quantity. The mouse jeered the lioness for bearing but a single cub. "True," replied the lioness, "and you have twelve, but my one is a lion." Xerxes had nearly two million soldiers, Leonidas three hundred. But the three hundred were Spartans. The Spirit of God was not poured out at Pentecost until the providence of God had so sifted the multitude, who waved palms before Jesus, that those who remained found room in a single upper chamber.

There were two churches in Scotland. One of them added to its membership two hundred and fifty converts in a single year, and rejoiced greatly in its growth. The other that same twelvemonth gained but a single member and lamented its barrenness. But the single member was David Livingston, and therefore in due time it appeared to all men that the " barren had borne seven, while she that had many children had waxed feeble."

Because quality counts for more than quantity a third sorting was required. Therefore Gideon led the ten thousand down to the brook of Jezreel, which flows at the base of the hill, in sight of the enemy, as if advancing to attack. At the stream he halted his men to drink. Those who drank as cattle drink he was told to send home. Those who drank as hounds drink were the men for the crisis.

Men show most certainly their essential characters in the trifles they do unconsciously, and the genius of leadership belongs to him who can see the meaning of signs which to others appear insignificant, and read, in the sparkle of white dust upon the surface, that gold-bearing quartz lies beneath. A hunter will most easily appreciate the exquisite accuracy of Gideon's test. But to any one who will watch a dog and a cow drink water, its purpose will grow plain.

Oxen fix their eyes upon the stream, glue

their lips to the water, and drink all they want, heedless of everything except the slaking of their thirst. You may pound them, but they will not move until they have had enough.

Dogs glance at the water, touch their tongues to it, but keep their eyes turning watchfully hither and thither, as if drinking seemed to them a trivial matter, and every sense must be kept alert to whatever of serious moment may occur. His tongue may be parched or swollen, none the less a dog always drinks as if slaking his thirst were a trifle to be instantly deferred if need be.

So the three hundred did not kneel upon the bank, but stood watching, and caught up the water in their hands, as if watching, and not drinking, were their business.

I. The attitude reveals concentration and persistency of purpose. Success in any cause depends in great degree upon having an aim and holding stanchly to it. Two young men begin life abreast. Both are poor; both are friendless; both are equally gifted. In twenty years one is at the top, the other at the foot, of the ladder, only because one has turned aside to gather flowers, to fly kites, or to sleep. The other has refused to be diverted from his aim.

Paul says he won the race, not because he was gifted, not because he was inspired, but because he kept his eyes fixed upon the goal. Gideon will have only men of one idea. That is what our Lord meant in declaring that unless we forsake all for Him we cannot be his disciples.

II. A dog drinking is the emblem of alertness. Watch him! If a leaf rustles, he sees it and starts. Sights and sounds which elude your powers of observation arrest his. He pauses, seems to consider; dashes away, circles around until assured that all is as it should be, then returns to resume his drinking. He may do this a dozen times before his thirst is quenched.

The successful man perceives every circumstance which bears upon the purpose of his life. Success is the right use of opportunities which pass us with the speed of wings never to return. Opportunity, says the Eastern proverb, has a beard, but no back hair. You may catch and hold it from before, but never from behind.

The French are being driven at Austerlitz, when Napoleon observes that the Russian columns are charging over a frozen lake. He orders his gunners to fire at the zenith. The descending balls pound the ice into fragments; the Russian column is destroyed, and so defeat is converted into that victory which Victor Hugo affirms to be the most brilliant known to history.

Paul walking the streets of Athens discerns an altar inscribed "To the Unknown God." Instantly, by making it a pulpit, he compels the brain of the world to listen for a season to the gospel.

III. Intensity of purpose, combined with alertness in detecting and employing opportunities, always gives a certain quality of character for which I cannot readily find a name, but which you may find exhibited by the next dog you see lapping from the gutter.

Even when the hound appears to hear nothing, to see nothing, he does not drink continuously. At intervals he pauses as if a thought, which he must consider, had struck him. He seems to be reflecting. An instant passes and he resumes his drinking.

There is this much of inspiration in all men. Our best thoughts, our most fertile suggestions, often come to us in moments when the mental powers are relaxed. If the mind is so trained that one's thoughts flow spontaneously in the channels cut for them by the main purpose of his life, his usefulest plans will be suggested to him at moments when he is not seeking them. Newton was strolling for rest when he observed the apple fall. James Watt was warming himself by the kitchen fire when he saw the steamboat in his mother's tea-kettle. Daniel Webster was on a pleasure trip, enjoying the prospect from the Heights of Abraham, and listening to the evening drum-beat of the British garrison at Quebec, when first occurred to him that magnificent description of English dominion as the empire on which the sun never sets, though years elapsed before the Senate was electrified by its utterance.

Here lies the arch peril of amusements. If a man allows himself to become so much absorbed in them, innocent though they may be, that in moments of relaxation his thoughts will gravitate towards them, he will rarely excel. If music is one's business, it is well when the grating of files sets him thinking how they may be tuned. But if the average man allows himself to become so interested in cards, or billiards, or operas, or horses, that when he is not compelled to think of his proper business he instinctively thinks of them, he will never give the world prime work.

IV. The most conspicuous distinction between the dog and the ox at water is this: the ox never heeds his master until his thirst is quenched; the dog never heeds his thirst till his master is obeyed. I have seen a hound panting with heat, his black lips baked, his tongue cracked, dart toward the cool spring. But his master's whistle arrests him at the brink, and he darts back without a drop. I have watched drovers call, pound, goad oxen at the ford, but the beasts would not budge until their thirst was slaked. Both types you may have seen among recruits enlisted in the army of the Lord.

If we should trace, step by step, the conflict in which the Midianites were defeated, we would see that the victory was won solely by the exercise on the part of Gideon's men of those qualities displayed in their drinking.

1. Oxen are bigger and stronger than dogs. The Midianites were many, the Is-

raelites were few. But a single purpose absorbed each of the three hundred. It was to reach a certain spot undiscovered.

2. To do that required them to keep their faculties almost preternaturally alert. They stole upon the foe, wary, watchful, every sense awake. It is dark. The crackling of a dry twig beneath a careless tread may give the alarm. It is night, and without hawks' eyes no man can be sure of his way.

3. But if the three hundred reach their goal, that will be futile unless they keep the lights burning within their pitchers. Each must watch his torch. He must guard it as one guards his secret thoughts. Ever and anon, as a dog who pauses from time to time we know not why, he must get sight of his candle without allowing a ray to escape in front.

4. Most important of all conditions of success, he must observe every sound and sign made by his leader, and be ready for instant obedience. A moment's delay in breaking the pitchers, blowing the trumpets, shouting the battle-cry when the signal had been given, would have converted the most brilliant victory of Hebrew annals into a pitiable fiasco.

If you will read with these suggestions the seventh chapter of Judges, it may grow plain why Cromwell's Ironsides, who never were defeated, with instinctive perception of its significance, selected for their battle-cry, the cry which heralded victory at Naseby and Marston Moor, "The sword of the Lord and of Gideon." It may also become apparent what qualities of character are requisite in us who would win in that more strenuous and important spiritual warfare we wage for Jesus Christ. "For we wrestle not with flesh and blood, but with principalities and powers."

VIII.

SELF-PITY: SAUL IN THE WITCH'S CAVE.

And Saul answered, I am sore distressed; for the Philistines make war against me, and God is departed from me, and answereth me no more, neither by prophets nor by dreams; therefore I have called thee, that thou mayest make known unto me what I shall do. — 1 SAM. xxviii. 15. (R. V.)

I DO not know whether I have been more thrilled by the horror, touched by the pathos, or numbed by the despair, in these words. They appear to be true. They were utterly false.

The horror of them is this: they express a man's deliberate conviction that God, in whom he lives and moves and has his being, has cast him off, and left him to struggle alone against forces which sweep him as Niagara sweeps a skiff.

The pathos of them is twofold. They are Saul's only complaint. They are the single shriek of one who believes himself a lost spirit pushed into the abyss. But they also express the awful loneliness of a human being famishing for sympathy. Because he thinks he cannot have God, Saul turns to Samuel. So I have seen a woman who had outlived her associates, or driven them away by persistent selfishness, turn to a poodle and try to make it fill the place of a friend! So I have heard men in stress of trouble entreat me to pray for them, without a thought of praying for themselves, because, while God was drawing them to his ear by their afflictions, they fancied God had departed from them.

The hopelessness of Saul's condition was that he mistook his own doings for God's, and, while the world was green and only his own glasses gray, fancied the world was gray and his glasses clear.

The apparent truth of Saul's words comes from the fact that he was alienated from God. Their essential falsehood is in their saying that God had deserted him, when in fact he had deserted God.

I. Recall the scene, — a valley three miles wide, running from northeast to southwest. Northward it swells upward into the hill Moreh. Its south side is Mount Gilboa. At the base of Gilboa flows the spring of

Jezreel, a stream fifty yards wide. Upon the plain, north and west of Gilboa, the Philistines are encamped. South of the stream, upon the north slope of Gilboa, are Saul and his army. There is no reason for supposing that his forces were outnumbered by the enemy. That enemy was the Philistines, and the Philistines he had defeated many times. His position was impregnable. He could choose his own time for attack, or decline battle altogether, for his base of supplies was immediately behind him, while the enemy were cut off from theirs and must fight or retreat. The strength of the Philistine army was in their iron chariots. These could only be employed upon the plain. They could not charge through the dense woods or up the steep slopes of Gilboa, upon the crest of which Saul's troops were safe as an eagle in its eyry. He was encamped on the spot whence Gideon descended upon the Midianites, and won the most brilliant battle recorded in the history of Israel. Every indication promised an easy and decisive victary, if only Saul could be Saul. But that he cannot be. Once he would have minded those Philistines as a lion minds jackals. But his courage is gone. He cannot hope, because he cannot pray. He feels that God has departed from him. Where clear eyes would have seen signs of promise, he discerns only signals of despair. What shall he do?

II. Seven miles as the bee flies north of his camp, directly in the rear of the Philistine army, lies Endor. At Endor lives a woman who claims that she can raise the dead. Perhaps she can. If so, it is by help of the infernal powers. If not, she is a fraud. In either case she is a wizard, and Saul himself has commanded that every wizard in the land be put to death. To this woman, whether fraud or fiend he may not know, but believing her to be the latter, Saul resolved to direct those prayers which he dares not address to God. Often you may see men, who count it folly to pray to the Almighty Love, turn with agony of supplication to fellow-mortals weaker or wickeder than themselves!

Disguising himself, in order both to elude the Philistine outposts and to deceive the woman by whom he will be deceived, he makes a wide detour around the hostile army, and next appears in the witch's cave.

It is night. Darkness and misery are friends to each other, but fiends to a guilty soul. Every step of the dark and dismal journey has taken something from Saul's manhood. Every step has quenched some ray of the light that still glimmers in his spirit, the light that lighteth every man that cometh into the world. He is moving from his friends. Every foot he advances brings more of his foes between his defenceless body and its natural protectors. He is going from his God. Every foot he advances brings more of tormenting memories between his soul and his heavenly Father. Inch by inch, he is going from the light toward the outer darkness. This he knows. Still he moves on. Have you never seen men walking from Gilboa to Endor?

III. At last the fearful journey ends. Whether correctly or not I do not know, and it does not in the least matter, for the Bible does not tell us, Saul believes himself in the presence of the spirit of the dead. Under the pressure of that tremendous conviction the inmost workings of his spirit appear. His secret thoughts break from him. Hitherto he has kept silence. But now the volcanic fires burst through the granite of his pride. The living who might have helped him have sought his confidence in vain. But into the ear of an impotent shade, a dead man powerless to help or hurt, he pours his despair like a lava flood.

"Why hast thou disquieted me to bring me up?" The question may have been the ventriloquism of a charlatan bribed by the Philistines to practise upon Saul's superstition, and meant to check further inquiry. It may have been some sign from the unseen world. Again I repeat, I do not know and it does not matter. But Saul believed that Samuel spoke, and the misery of it is, he believed that Samuel could love him when God had ceased to care for him; he believed there could be rain upon the grass when there was no water in the sea. Therefore his reply: "I am sore distressed; for the Philistines make war upon me, and God is departed from me and answereth me no more, neither by prophets nor by dreams. Therefore I have called thee up, that thou mayest make known to me what I ought to do."

This, then, is what Saul has been thinking. These are the thoughts which have driven him, as they will drive any man who cherishes them, to the chamber of death, the wizard's cave, the ante-room of hell.

And what were the facts that corresponded to Saul's fancies? Statement by statement, word for word, accurately and absolutely, the reverse of what Saul imagines them to be, says that they are.

"I am sore distressed." The words mean, "I am pressed upon from without" by untoward events, as a weight presses upon a body and crushes it.

The fact was the opposite, as we have seen. Saul was sore rent from within. Conscious of his pain, he attributes its origin not in the least to the real cause, which was himself, but to something outside his own soul which he had not caused and could not cure, and for which he was not responsible. He is shaking with ague and thinks that it is winter, though the air is warm upon his cheeks.

"For the Philistines make war upon me." It was he who had inaugurated war upon the Philistines, and incurred their desperate and implacable hostility by compelling David to a deed of wanton and disgusting cruelty upon them. Not only that. Even now the Philistines would not have dared to rise in arms against him but for this. David had been Saul's most brilliant soldier and his ablest captain. By him again and again the Philistines had been routed. While David fought for Israel, the Philistines had not ventured to begin even movements for self-defence. But Saul in his frantic jealousy had banished David, and thus given the Philistines hope and courage to attack him.

"And God has departed from me." Had God moved? Saul had moved, from the shrine at Shiloh, where God showed himself in light, to the darkness of a witch's cave. While the Father's arms are stretched out all the day long, saying, "Why wilt thou die?" the child runs from Him lamenting, "My Father has cast me off!"

"And answereth me no more." There, were three ways in which Saul knew that God communed with him and answered his requests, — by dreams or visions, by prophets, by Urim.

1. By dreams. The narrative relates how in Saul's younger days music had exerted a mysterious power upon him, and brought him into a state of spiritual exaltation in which inspired visions came to him. We

are also told that he had driven away from his presence, by attempting to murder him, the only man whose harp had power to exert that mysterious influence upon him. Thus he had closed, and still held closed, one of the three doors by which it was possible for God to answer him.

2. By prophets. Saul had driven from his presence Samuel, the greatest of the prophets, by persistent disobedience, and had withdrawn from the lesser prophets who remained. Thus he had himself closed the second door of divine communication.

3. There was a third method in which God had been accustomed to make known his will. It was communion by Urim. What this was we do not know. It was in some way connected with the gleam of a precious stone, probably a diamond, worn by the high priest, and the mysterious communication could come only through the priest acting as mediator. But Saul, in a frenzy of wrath against David, had slaughtered all the members of the priestly house save one, and that one was in exile, still under sentence of death.

Thus Saul had locked the three doors, the only three of which he knew, by which

God could answer him, and held the keys of them in his hand at the moment when he cried in despair, "God answereth me no more." Was Saul, in this insanity of self-delusion, wholly unlike us?

IV. There is one other point in Saul's exclamation which I would have you observe.

What an energy of anguish throbs in the two words "no more"! — "God answers me no more." Saul appreciates the awfulness of the change which has occurred in his relations toward God, though he is so wildly oblivious of the cause. He sees the great gulf fixed between himself in torment and the water for one drop of which he pleads, though he does not see by whom the gulf has been fixed. He burns in the flames he has kindled, though he thinks God has kindled them to consume him. He pleads with Abraham for one drop of water, without a suspicion that God's bosom, an ocean, is there for him to lie upon. He has gone the way of those who love not the truth, upon whom has been sent "a strong delusion that they should believe a lie."

"No more." It was not always so. Once he could turn to God with hope and joy. Once peace brooded over him. The light in the past makes the darkness of the present more appalling, as a sailor drowning in the night sees afar the candle shining in the cottage of the mother he has forsaken. It is the sight of a little child kneeling by the white crib and falling asleep as he prays — asleep in trust and peace — that compels a wicked man to realize his loneliness, even if it does not force him to appreciate his guilt. Once he was a little child! Once he could pray and sleep like that. But now! If he seeks help from the invisible powers, and there are times when all men do that, he can turn only to the wizards that peep and mutter, and pretend they can change the laws of the Almighty.

It is plain, I think, why there could be no hope for Saul, no deliverance from misery for him, while he remained in such a spirit. You or I, beholding agony like his, though in our bitterest foe, would have whispered words of hope. But God is kinder than we. There was no hope until Saul himself should change. Only the truth can make men free. Therefore the truth was spoken to him. He was reminded of the past, reminded that only those things had come upon him which he had been assured would come if he went the way he had gone. He was reminded of Moses and the prophets, and warned to hear them, and told that he had but a night to listen. No gleam of hope from any outward change was given him. "To-morrow thou and thy sons shall be with me."

However these words were spoken, whether by fraud or by miracle, God permitted them. How they affected Saul we are not told. After this single outburst of despair the monarch resumed the majesty of silence. He wrapped his curse about him and went forth into the night. The next day he fought bravely, he died not ignobly, and when men begin to do well I infer that it has begun to go well with them. But this I know: every pang Saul felt, every loss he endured, every star that was extinguished in his sky, marked a fresh effort of God to open his blind eyes and his deaf ears, that he might see and hear and perceive who had kindled and kept aflame the fires that consumed him, till he should turn to Him who was saying then and is saying still, "Come unto me, all ye that labor and are heavy laden, and I will give you rest."

IX.

SAMSON: SELF-DECEPTION.

And it came to pass, when she pressed him daily with her words, and urged him, so that his soul was vexed unto death, that he told her all his heart, and said unto her, There hath not come a razor upon mine head; for I have been a Nazarite unto God from my mother's womb: if I be shaven, then my strength will go from me, and I shall become weak, and be like any other man. — JUDGES xvi. 16, 17.

SAMSON is perhaps the most fascinating character described in the Old Testament. His biography exhilarates the reader. We admire his courage, exult in his strength, are charmed by his good-nature. Dean Stanley, guided by the fine exegetical insight of Professor Ewald, has taught us to recognize in this champion of Dan " the solitary humorist " of sacred history, and to believe that though " he was capable of every crime but cowardice," he was also " capable of every virtue but humility." It is easy to palliate the vices and exaggerate the excellences of a character so captivating. Men pardon excesses in a good-natured man who makes them laugh. When they see one who never backbites, nor envies, nor hesitates to squander his money; who is kind to his friends and fearless of his foes; going the broad way which obviously leads to ruin, they are wont to say, " He is a noble fellow;" " He is his own worst enemy." They forget that the same is true of those who do not pass for "noble fellows;" that Iago, no less than Othello, was "his own worst enemy."

We are drawn to Samson because he always appears with a smile upon his face. We can hear his boisterous laughter as he stands upon the hill that overlooks the Philistine plain, and watches the frightened jackals scampering through the fields of ripe grain, scattering fire as they run. We can detect the sly smile of smothered mirth, as with lamb-like meekness he permits himself to be bound and delivered to his foes. We wait without anxiety, with curiosity alone, until he breaks his bonds, as one breaks tow that fire has scorched, and smites his captors hip and thigh, shouting out the would-be pun, " With the jaw of an ass I have slain a mass." A poor pun it is, but a vent sufficing for his rollicking humor. He has all our sympathy when, rising at midnight, he steps carefully over the sleeping Philistines' guards who are waiting to arrest him at dawn; unhinges the leaves of the city gates, and lugs them on his burly shoulders, like a school-boy sweating to accomplish a practical joke, three miles, to the crest of the hill, where all in Gaza must see them in the morning. When he bends between the pillars of Dagon's temple, his irrepressible humor breaks forth in a last grim jest, even in prayer: "Give me strength just this once to be avenged for *one* of my two eyes." For

——"when he died his parting groan
Had more of laughter than of moan."

For more than twenty years this jovial, mighty man of valor "judged Israel." During the whole of that period he was never conquered until he told his secret. To see him then, bound in fetters of brass, in the prison-house of his repulsive foes, —

"Eyeless, in Gaza, at the mill, with slaves!" —

the sunny Samson blind; the champion of Israel at Gaza; the resistless warrior in prison; the strongest of men doing woman's work; the breaker of fetters wearing them;

all on account of a moment's amiable weakness; all because the great, strong, brave, generous heart could not resist a woman's crocodile tears — this seems too mournful. It seems monstrous, a thing that ought not to have been.

Yet such is, I think, substantially the general estimate of Samson and of his career. We weigh him in the same scales in which society weighs the noble young men whom every one loves, and who would be so useful to the world, with their rare gifts, such ornaments to the community, if only they would not get drunk, nor gamble, nor break the hearts of their wives and mothers; if only they had not been overcome by temptation in moments of weakness, stolen the funds of the men who trusted them, and squandered the hardly earned savings of other people in buying fine horses and building palaces for themselves.

I think we are wise in going to this episode with Delilah for the explanation of Samson's ruin. But I doubt whether the current reading of that episode is exhaustive, and therefore I would have you read it once more.

1. And first I would have you observe

that the scene described in the text occurred, not at the beginning, but at the close, of Samson's career. For nearly twenty years he had been at his work. Yet by his strength and his courage, by his battles, his jokes, and his various activities, he had accomplished literally less than nothing of the task he had been appointed to perform, the task to which he had deliberately dedicated his life. That task, assigned to him by God, revealed through an angel, accepted first by his parents and then by himself, was the liberation of his country from Philistine oppression. Twenty years have passed since Samson, endowed with superhuman powers, began his judgeship. Still his people are not free. At his death the Philistines will be stronger than they were at his birth, and their chains more firmly riveted upon Israel. Near the close of the twenty years Samson himself is lying supine upon the breast of the ablest, the most patriotic, and the most fascinating of Philistine women. Surely something must be wrong; something for which Delilah alone is not responsible; something which cannot be explained by the theory of a moment's amiable weakness in Samson himself.

SAMSON: SELF-DECEPTION. 117

2. Observe, when Samson yielded to an irrational impulse and revealed his secret, he only did once more what he had been doing all his life.

There are two types of men. The first are controlled by principle, the second by impulse. The first live the life of God. The second live the life of beasts.

A cat scratches when she feels like scratching, and purrs when she feels like purring. When she scratches, we smite her; when she purrs, we pet her. A snake hisses, a dove coos. We kill snakes, we cherish doves. But a man who does well only "when he feels like it" is in training to do ill "when he feels like" doing that. While he lives the life of the dove, he is equally living the life of the cat, of the snake. Samson was such a man. There is not an act recorded of him which he did not perform simply because he "felt like doing it." He had been intrusted with an important mission. He had been furnished with abilities adequate to its demands. He was allowed twenty years to complete his work. Instead of setting himself to do it, like a man, because it was given him to do, he worked only when the impulse seized him, — when it was therefore easier for him to work than to play. Thus even the right things he did — if such can be found recorded, of which I am not sure — trained him steadily to be more and more the slave of his impulses; and when at last the impulse to do obviously wrong came upon him, he obeyed it precisely as an untrained cat scratches, and an untrained horse kicks.

The essential blasphemy against God in whose image we are made, the crime against nature for us who have been created men and not brutes, has been committed by the man who says, "I will do as I like;" "I will do this just because I feel like doing it;" "I will leave that undone just because I do not feel like doing it."

That fact explains why the magnificent Samson was at last compelled to grind meal in the mills of his enemies, though the sordid and servile Jacob came in due time to be the prince of Israel.

3. The life of impulse in men always tends to become the life of self-deception.

The text shows us how profound was the deception which Samson practised upon himself.

Intentional deceit is the vice of the weak.

SAMSON: SELF-DECEPTION. 119

Foxes and little children and slaves, who have no other weapons of defence, take instinctively to lying. But there are curves so large that they seem flat. The world is round, yet to us who live upon it the world seems a plain. Such was Samson's curve from the straight line of truth.

In my childhood I was suffered to believe that so long as the Danite hero persisted in telling lies to Delilah he was safe, while the instant he whispered the truth he was lost. An unwholesome moral that, especially for children, even if it were taught in the Bible. But it is not taught in the Bible; least of all is it taught here.

Samson said, "If they bind me with green withes I shall be as another man." That every child perceives to be a lie. "If they bind me with new ropes." That, too, is obviously a falsehood. "If my locks are weaved together." That was no less evidently a deception. But what every child who reads this narrative should be made to understand is this: when Samson told Delilah "all that was in his heart," that is, when he uttered to her his profoundest conviction, and said, "I have been a Nazarite from my youth," he spoke perhaps the largest lie that exists in recorded literature, though he had so warped his conscience that he believed it to be a truth. The penalty of persistent. lying is loss of ability to discern the truth.

Samson knew perfectly well what a Nazarite was. An angel had explained the meaning of the word to his parents before he was born. It was clearly defined in the laws of Moses. His father and mother reminded him of its significance when, in his first recorded action, he refused to heed its meaning.

A Nazarite was one set apart by God for a peculiar mission, who accepted the mission and renounced the world, with all its pleasures, in order to devote his energies, undistracted by the common allurements or cares of life, to the vocation to which he had been called. As a sign that he accepted his appointed work, the Nazarite was required to abstain from wine, and to wear his hair uncut; indications that he had no leisure to enjoy the ordinary gratifications or conform to the current customs of society. These outward signs, the long hair and the abstinence from wine, were merely door-plates announcing that a devoted and self-denying spirit dwelt within. Samuel was a Nazarite.

John the Baptist was a Nazarite: But there was no need of mentioning their long hair to advertise the fact. Their lives evinced it. But Samson was the worldliest of the worldly. Year after year he lived the most obvious falsehood, a falsehood proclaimed by his unshorn locks to every eye that beheld him. His long hair said: "This is a man who sacrifices himself, yields every personal desire, every personal interest, every pleasure this world can give, every hope and every fear, to a divinely given mission." Yet not one deed is recorded of this long-haired man which was not done to gratify some personal passion, some personal vanity, or some personal impulse. Torquemada in the Spanish inquisition is certainly a repulsive object in our eyes, and Samson, even in his wild excesses of good humor, seems attractive to us. But Torquemada, kindling fires to burn those he hates, and calling himself a disciple of Jesus because he wears a red cross embroidered upon his black robe, was not a more colossal fraud than Samson devoting his life to the gratification of his whims, his vanity, and his lusts, while he called himself a Nazarite because he wore long hair. It was time his hair should be cut, time that he who had so thoroughly deceived himself, should at last be taught the truth. Be sure it was not his veracity, but his living and speaking a lie, which caused his ruin.

4. This sunny Samson, whom we have all admired so much; from whose sorrows we cannot withhold our sympathy; in whom Milton saw the tragedy of his own heroic life foreshadowed, and Handel recognized a prototype; with whom Ewald has taught us to laugh and Stanley to rejoice, appears to have been but a sham hero after all. Essentially, beneath the splendid clothes he wore, he seems to have been an altogether selfish and paltry creature. What act of his has been recorded which he did not do for his own sake?

He fell in love with a Philistine woman. Thwarted in his love, he attacked and slew the men who had thwarted him. That was his first obedience to the Nazarite vow which bound him to devote his life, without sharing the common passions of mankind, solely to the emancipation of his country.

Provoked by a personal injury, he declared, "I will be avenged," and set fire to the cornfields of those with whom he was angry. That was his second act of obedience to the Nazarite vow. Besieged in Gaza by men who sought his life, he arose at midnight, and wasted his great strength lugging the city gates to place them where they would advertise his prowess. This prank, which exasperated without weakening the foes of his country, was the third act of obedience to his Nazarite vow.

When bound hand and foot, and surrounded by his own vindictive enemies, he broke the ropes that bound him, and slew a thousand men to save his own life. Of all these amazing efforts not one was inspired by patriotism or the memory of his vow; and when at last the inevitable end of such a career had come, his dying prayer, as he bent between the pillars, was not for his country, but for himself: "O Lord, that I may be avenged upon the Philistines."

Is it not plain why Samson's life was futile?

Why, then, is it that the career of Samson fascinates us, and why do we find it difficult to blame him? If he was the slave of his passions, a false man, a wholly selfish, trivial man, why do we not despise him?

I will answer that question by asking another. Why do men admire Byron, Aaron Burr, and Napoleon? And why is it woe to the disciples of Christ when all men speak well of them?

X.

TO PARENTS.

Train up a child in the way he should go, and when he is old he will not depart from it. — PROV. xxii. 6.

THE text may have originated with Solomon. If so, it contains the judgment of the most observant and sagacious of men. More probably it was a proverb in Israel, and therefore expresses the general judgment of the race which has trained its children more admirably than any other which has yet appeared on earth.

When Waltham would make watches it went to Geneva for instruction. For the same reason wise parents turn to the Bible for guidance in family discipline.

I. The example of Solomon warns us to remember that those who do not govern themselves, cannot govern their children. In this respect the celebrated epigram upon Charles II.,

"Who never said a foolish thing,
And never did a wise one,"

may be applied to the wise king of Israel.

We do not know that any of Solomon's sons turned out well, and yet the most judicious maxims for parents that can be found have come to us through him.

The background of the text, therefore, warns us that the first essential in the government of our children is the government of ourselves. Rehoboam did not obey his father's precepts; he imitated his father's example.

A large part of parental discipline must consist in rewards and punishments. God's government is full of them. Every act of obedience to his law is rewarded; every act of disobedience is punished. But the divine punishments are administered without a tinge of passion. If one lies he will suffer. If one gets drunk his head will ache. These penalties are inexorable. But the drunkard feels that he suffers not because God is angry with him, but because he has dashed himself against a law.

When parents punish children, it is often only bad temper at work. The boy has been forbidden to throw stones. He throws twenty, and nothing is done. The twenty-first breaks a window-pane, and he is disciplined with perhaps undue enthusiasm.

He knows he is made to suffer, not because he has broken a law, but because he has broken a window. He thinks his father "outrageous" to care so much for a bit of glass, and his opinion is indisputably correct.

A child by his fretful ways makes the house a purgatory until his mother's patience is exhausted. Then she boxes his ears, and so makes him realize, not that she can govern him, but that she cannot govern herself.

A man burned down his house by trying to govern his stove before he had learned to govern himself. The weather was cold and the coal would not burn. He shook out the ashes. He grew hot and red. The lever slipped and bruised his fingers. It slipped again and bruised them worse. Then the grate stuck fast. He caught the lever with both hands, braced both feet, and jerked it viciously. Of course the stove was upset, the hot coals rolled upon the floor, and he shouted for assistance. The stove cared nothing for his temper. It obeyed its own laws. When the man lost his temper, he could not perceive those laws. But the safety of his house depended upon his obeying them.

The laws which govern the human spirit

are as inexorable, and far more occult and complex, than those which govern stoves. A man in temper is always blind to them. He can better afford to burn up twenty houses than one home. Yet often have I been called to help put out the fire when the parent's temper had upset the child.

There is a false principle, sometimes deliberately adopted by parents, which works nearly as much disaster as bad temper itself; which is in fact the cosey nest in which bad temper often hatches its eggs, secure from attacks of conscience. It is this: "I have but one law with my children. That is, absolute, instant obedience to my command. Even when I have given an order which it would have been wiser not to have given, I exact unquestioning obedience, for the parent's authority must be preserved; and if a child once is allowed to question the wisdom of my commands, the foundations of family government will be undermined."

This is simply retaining in the household a legal fiction which has long been rejected from every civil government except perhaps in Russia and Turkey. It used to be said and believed, "The king can do no wrong." That fiction has cost many a sovereign both crown and head. It was blown into fragments, with memorable solemnities, by the French Revolution. The certain way to convince the people that their king can do no right, has been found to be, insisting that he can do no wrong. Parents who are not fools know that they are fallible. If they try to teach their children otherwise, they try to teach what they know is not true; and, in this world, no good ever comes of lying. The instant a parent finds himself in the wrong, he should confess the fact to his child. That is the one sure way of establishing and maintaining his authority.

I knew a child of exceptionally quick and strenuous impulses. Though affectionate he was not obedient, and needed to be watched as a weasel to be kept from mischief. His father told him to pick up a pin. The father thought the boy refused, but the father was mistaken. A sharp rebuke. The boy began to sulk (I had far rather hear a child swear than see him sulk). "Come here, sir!" The child did not stir. The father lost his temper. He seized his boy tempestuously; carried him into another room for punishment. The moment's delay brought the man to himself. He sat for a little while with his child in his arms. Then said: "My son, we have done wrong. I have lost my temper and you have lost yours. It is worse for me to do that than it is for you, because I am bigger and stronger and ought to be wiser than you. I ask God to forgive me and I ask you. I must be right before I can help you to be right. Help me to be a good father, so that I can help you to be a good son." The sullen defiance left the child's face. His arms clasped his father's neck. "Father, I didn't say what you thought I did!" The child was six years old. He is now sixteen. The father is a quick-tempered man. But I have heard him say repeatedly that, for ten years, he has never had occasion to rebuke his boy, by word or gesture, for the slightest approach to disobedience. The man of fifty and the boy of sixteen appear to live and have their being in each other as a single soul.

It is sometimes urged: "But the child's will must be broken. Unless that is done he will surely come to grief."

Break a child's will! You had better break his back. The parent's chief business is to strengthen his child's will. Will power means success both in this life and in the life which is to come. Men become drunkards because they lack will power. They fail in their vocations; they sink into idleness and pauperism and all manner of ruinous self-indulgences, because their wills are weak. They do not become Christians, or they continue paltry, useless Christians, because they have so little will power.

A kitten is born blind and weak of limb. Nature prepares it to be a good cat not by breaking its weak little claws, but by opening its blind little eyes. The parents' business is not to make children do what is right, which for a time is easy and then impossible, but to make them will what is right, which at first is difficult, but if achieved becomes instinctive.

Johnnie has disobeyed. You said he should not play with the carving knife, and there it is in his hand. It is there because his will is weak, not as you fancy because his will is strong. When you told him not to do it, there was in him a little bit of resolution to obey you, because he loves you. But the resolution was not strong enough to resist temptation. Your business is to strengthen his weak will until it becomes stronger than anything that can attack it.

There are a hundred different ways of doing this, and the study of your life should be to find them. You may conquer the child a thousand times, and each time you have injured him unless you have helped him to conquer himself. Every child, even when in a fury, is a little Paul. He feels, though he cannot say, " Wretched child that I am. That which I would not I do, and that which I would I do not. Who shall deliver me from the body of this death." You, the parent, are set by God to deliver him by strengthening his will.

II. How to do this the text can teach us.

1. By training the child " in the way he *should* go."

Avoid training him in the way he ought not to go. The babe lies quietly in his little crib. His soft eyes wander over the room. He is studying hard. He begins to smile and coo. He is obeying the sweetest impulses that can sway the human spirit. Wise mothers select this moment to whisper in his ears murmurs of approval and endearment. They let other matters wait while they smile upon their darling. Foolish mothers let him lie without a word. They are too busy to notice, and are only thankful that the child is quiet. But when he grows weary and begins to kick and scream, they hasten to caress him, and call him "mother's precious darling." So in politics and in churches it not infrequently occurs, that a man may continue until he dies doing all things, bearing all things, sacrificing all things for the general good, sweet spirited as Stephen, while none praise, none observe, except to use him for their own selfish ends. But the instant he grows fractious and hateful *enough*, all begin to pet and truckle to him for fear of what he may do next. They even put him in office, not because he is fit for the place, but to keep him in good temper.

Babies are by no means fools. When they get petted for kicking and neglected for smiling they draw influential inferences.

It should be remembered that when, at the beginning of his career, a healthy child screams or frets, it is always pins or colic. If it is pins, remove them. If colic, send for the physician. If it is because you have trained him to disturb the household by his temper, you must undo your work.

The wisest and tenderest mother I ever knew, a mother loved so dearly that when she had been a year in heaven her youngest child, only eight years old, was heard saying: "We must take care to remember what mother said, because if we make her sorry now she cannot tell us!" made it an inflexible rule that her children should never have anything for which they cried. Before most parents would have supposed them old enough to understand her meaning, she carefully explained to them that in this world no one ever gets anything by whining for it; at least no one ought to, and they certainly would not. Her teaching was effective.

Again, when a child trips or stumbles and hurts himself, have you never heard, "Naughty chair to trip baby! Mamma whip chair." It is easy in that fashion to dry up tears! But it is drying them by kindling the fires of hell. It is planting seeds whose harvests appear in the moody man who blames circumstances for the results of his own transgressions. Is it not as easy to rouse the sweet side of the child's nature by working through his imagination; to say, "Poor chair! Baby hurt chair. Mamma kiss chair and make it well." That is to dry tears by the sun of heaven.

A hundred illustrations are at hand.

Perhaps the commonest is this. A child snatches at table. "Why, my son! Suppose company were here! What would Mrs. B—— think if she saw you do that!"

So the principle of conduct which Christ vehemently denounced is instilled into the receptive spirit, and the little one is taught to " do all things to be seen of men." The child is forced to feel that the opinions of strangers are more important than the happiness of his parents and sisters. Thus; for as those who know tell us that before a human being is three years old it learns more than it ever acquires after that age, though it should live to be a hundred; and as the child is father of the man; a crop is sown of husbands who will be polite to every one's wife except their own; of fathers and brothers who will suppress their tempers in society, and let them effervesce at home.

2. We are told to train a child in the " way he should *go*."

But many train them to stand still. It is a child's nature " to go," and go he will. Right or wrong he will go!

A common mistake, and a fatal one, is made by those who endeavor to mould children by negatives.

God begins their training by prompting them to incessant activity. They never rest save when they are sick or asleep.

Parents are often satisfied with telling children what they must not do. Long ago Milton wrote that one ounce of right doing was worth many pounds of forcible prevention of wrong doing. I suppose most of us have reproved our little ones twenty times for doing what we did not want them to do, for once that we have praised them for doing as we wished to have them. Who watches and when the child has tried twenty times in vain to make his card house stand, cries out "Bravo!" when at the twenty-first attempt his perseverance succeeds? The way to prevent a child from doing wrong things is to encourage him in doing right ones.

A parent should be a governor in the mechanical meaning of that word. He should be a great fly-wheel. When the little wheels work too fast, it gathers up the superfluous energy. When they flag, it restores the hoarded force, and thus keeps them all moving evenly, but moving. Most of us perform the least important part of the duty. We check the disturbing energy, especially when our heads ache, but we do not give it back to impel the children forward in good works.

3. To train a child in the way he should go is often a different matter from training him in the way we wish he would go.

There are certain not over wise maxims which have been over much believed. Such are these: that the child is blank paper, upon which the parent may write what he likes; that as the twig is bent the tree is inclined; that the child is virgin soil, in which you may plant what seed you choose, sure that it will bear fruit after its kind.

Parents who think so are like to reap fine crops from their virgin soil! The child is a field in which ancestors have been planting seeds for thousands of years. That small bundle of impotence in your cradle is full of germs as a tropic jungle. Your business is to watch them, to cultivate the flowers and train the weeds, remembering that every weed has its uses. Tares and wheat will show their blades. We must recognize them when they appear. All the educational steam-pumps in the universe will never force into a child anything of which God has not put the germ within him. We can create nothing. We can only educate, that is, "draw out" into strength and beautiful growths what is already there.

Watch, and wait, and pray. Nothing will come up which wise and patient culture cannot train to useful manhood; even the tares can be made to fertilize the wheat. That boy is sly, secretive, deceitful. But this badness is only the untrained fruit of caution. Watched with sufficient care, it may be made the useful helper of frankness and valor.

4. To train a child in the way *he* should go is not to train him as other children should go.

This is the reason why there appears so often one black sheep in the flock. Parents are sometimes spoiled by their success with one child, until reformed by their failure with another. They think they have only to cast each child into the same candle mould which shaped their first so well.

But children are born to go different ways. The master in a menagerie trains each animal according to its nature. He does not try to make a falcon swim, or a fish fly, or an otter climb. But the distinctions between children are no less radical, and far more subtle and difficult to discern. Parents should remember that because they have succeeded with one child they are in danger of failing with another. Teaching a chicken to scratch does not qualify for teaching a duck to swim, except in the general way that it trains the trainer to be patient, persistent, and watchful. In certain respects all animals are similar, and all children are alike. If you show temper to animals, all will exhibit temper in return. But each in a different way. One will bite, another will scratch, another will kick, another will run away. If you are kind and just, all will respond and try to do your bidding, but each in its own fashion.

To the lay eye these larvæ look substantially alike. To it small differences in shade and size seem immaterial. But at a glance the naturalist declares, "That will be a white miller, give it grape leaves to eat; that will be a silk moth, give it mulberry; and that will be a purple emperor, feed it upon oak."

If men would observe their children, upon whose welfare their most precious hopes depend, with half the judicious care they have bestowed upon beasts and birds and fishes and insects, great would be their reward.

XI.

SAVING FAITH.

To Children.

Believe in the Lord Jesus Christ and thou shalt be saved. — Acts xvi. 31.

This promise was made to a man in great trouble. The man learned to believe in the Lord Jesus Christ and was saved from his trouble.

The words are as true for us to-day as they were for that man eighteen hundred years ago. Our troubles may be great or small. They may come from having the measles; from not getting what we want; from losing our friends, or from having to do what we don't like. Whatever they are, if we believe in the Lord Jesus Christ we shall be saved from them every one.

Not very many days ago there was a little boy in such distress that he could not eat his breakfast. When he tried to, his head dropped upon his plate, and he sobbed as if his heart would break. He had behaved badly in school. His teacher had sent a note to his father. He was mortified and miserable. His sobs asked as plainly as words, "What shall I do to be saved?"

Something within him said, "Teacher was mean as dirt to tell father! Pay her back. Be as hateful as you can without getting docked. Believe in *me*."

His father answered, "Jesus says *you* have been mean. He tells us when we have injured any one to confess it, and ask their pardon. Believe in *Him*, my boy, and you will be saved."

The little fellow went to school. "Teacher," he said, "I'm ashamed I acted so you had to tell father. I'm sorry, and I will try to be a good boy." He said this aloud like a man. All the boys heard him. He expected they would laugh at him and call him a sneak. But they did n't. His misery and tears departed as the fog goes before the sun. It was the happiest morning he ever spent in school.

This boy believed in the Lord Jesus and was saved from *his* trouble.

I. The Bible tells us that Jesus cannot save us unless we believe in Him. I wish you would stop a moment and think that out.

God gave you a mother. Without her care you would have died almost as soon as you were born. She fed you, dressed you, kept you warm, and saved you from a thousand perils of which you knew nothing, before you could do anything to help yourself.

So God has given you a Saviour, Jesus Christ. You cannot know a thousandth part of what He has done for you and is doing for you all the time.

But there are many things, and they are the worst things, from which a mother cannot save her child unless he believes in her.

When Charlie began to creep his mother told him not to go near the fire or it would hurt him. But Charlie's eyes told him a different story. They said, "The flame is kind and beautiful; go catch it. Perhaps you can make it sing like a bird." Charlie believed in his eyes, not in his mother, and the flame did not long seem lovely to him. Another time his mother caught her unbelieving boy before he reached the grate. He screamed and struggled to get away from her. He grew angry and hot. That too was misery for him. She could save him from being burnt outside, but she could not keep the fire from burning him inside, because he did not believe in her.

So you see a mother cannot save her child from misery, even by holding him in her arms and kissing him, unless he believes in her. But when he trusts her more than he trusts himself, believes her eyes and thoughts rather than his own, the fire will not hurt, it will help him. He will get its warmth and beauty without its sting. For folks are like trees, the things they believe are their roots, and the things they do their fruits.

Trusting Jesus' eyes and ears and thoughts more than our own St. Paul called "walking by faith." And Jesus himself called it "Believing in Him."

II. It is not easy to believe in Jesus. If it were the Bible would not spend so much time urging us to do it. For people do not need much urging to do easy things, but hard ones.

Even the things we see with our eyes are often so different from what they seem, that it is hard to believe the truth about them. Our eyes say the sun moves and the earth stands still. When my father told me how

SAVING FAITH. 143

the earth rolled round I did not believe him, because I thought the chimneys would tumble off the houses and the water out of the wells every night if what he said were true. But when we come to things we cannot see it is harder still to believe the truth. We are like travellers in a strange country who know neither the way nor the language, and do not see things as they are, but call stones bread, and gall honey, and poison water. There is something inside us always saying black is white, and bitter is sweet. If we believe *it* we get into no end of trouble here, and if we keep on believing it we shall be in misery always in this world and the next, for everything — even the kindest things, health and wealth and Christmas and friends — will hurt us.

But Jesus understands everything, and always tells us the truth about it. If we believe in Him all things, even the hatefullest, sickness and poverty and enemies, will help us. Therefore the first business of a wise boy or man will be to learn what Jesus calls things, and believe *that;* to learn what Jesus tells us, and do *that.*

Many a boy thinks, "If I had a velocipede, a pony, and a sail-boat; if I could have everything I want by wishing for it; if I never had to do anything I don't like, I should be happy."

Almost everybody in the world thinks the same. People do not often say it, but they act it, and Jesus tells us always to judge what a man believes by what he does and not by what he says. Most of the misery in the world comes from people's thinking they can be made happy by getting what they want and doing what they like. It is not true. Every one who tries finds out some time that it is false. Your father can tell you of men who have everything money can buy, who are able to do as they please, and yet are not half so happy as they used to be when they were children and had to live in a poor little house with scarcely enough to eat.

Jesus says we can be happy only through loving God and our neighbors. If we do that we shall be glad, whether we are rich or poor, sick or well. Neither father nor mother can tell you of any one who has tried Jesus' way and found that He was mistaken.

III. Believing in Jesus is a habit. We cannot believe in Him once for all and have it over like being vaccinated. We must acquire the habit little by little, day by day, just as we learn to walk or skate or believe in our mothers. We believed in them first of all because we loved them. But our faith grew stronger as we found that, whenever we thought differently from them, they were always right and we were always wrong.

But some one is ready to say : " I thought being saved always meant in the Bible going to heaven when we die ; and all your sermon is about this world ! "

In thinking so you are partly right and partly wrong. That kind of believing which does not help us out of trouble and into happiness in this world will not help us into heaven when we die. But if you learn to believe in the Lord Jesus so that He saves you from misery in this world, something will happen to you even better than going to heaven when you die. You will find yourself in heaven before you die. That is what Jesus promised. A little girl looked up and longed for the beautiful blue sky. I told her she was in the sky already, only she did not know it. Every time she breathed she swallowed some of the sky. In it she lived and moved and had her being as truly as the birds. When she held her breath — as she did once in a passion — her ears hummed, her head ached, and she grew black in the face just because she would not let the sky get into her, though it tried to all the time. So Jesus told a great many people they were in heaven, only they did not know it, and never would know it until they believed in Him. This He said to Nicodemus, a rich ruler; to a poor ignorant woman in Samaria; and to Mary and Martha when their brother was dead.

When we die we shall still be in heaven. When worms become butterflies they have the same air and sun as when they were worms, only they enjoy the sun and air a great deal more, because they themselves are changed.

So when we die we shall have the same God in whom we are living now. The same Jesus who is the light of this world will be the light of that world. If we cannot rejoice in the light here we shall not rejoice in Him there.

IV. Finally, Jesus says that if we will do as He tells us we will believe in Him, because He has made us so that we cannot help it.

You can try the truth of his words this minute if you like.

Perhaps mother has been reading this sermon aloud to you. It would not be strange if you were tired. Perhaps she is tired too. Ask her. Say, "Mother, let me read to you! I will read anything you like, and I'll try my best to read well."

"That's too much trouble," says self. "Do as you would be done by," says Jesus. Try Him, and see what comes of obeying Him.

Perhaps it is Sunday. The day seems long and tedious. "I wish father would tell me a story." "Whatsoever ye would that men should do unto you do you even so unto them," says Jesus. But you don't know any story! Then learn one. Take your Bible and learn this story of Paul and the jailer. Learn it so well that father will enjoy hearing you tell it.

If you cannot yourself remember anything Jesus tells you to do, ask your mother to repeat some command of his. Then do it at once with all your might. You will find that you cannot help believing in Him, and you will find you are in heaven. You will understand, too, better than all the preachers in the world can explain it, the meaning of the text: "Believe in the Lord Jesus Christ and thou shalt be saved."

XII.

FRANKLIN SNOW.

Covet earnestly the best gifts. — 1 Cor. xii. 31.
And now abideth faith, hope, charity, these three; but the greatest of these is charity. — 1 Cor. xiii. 13.
Follow after charity. — 1 Cor. xiv. 1.

WHILE urging men to desire the best gifts the Apostle is careful to remind them what the best gifts are. Among them he does not mention any of the things which most of us spend our lives in seeking, but those only which, when our lives are spent, we shall wish we had spent them in obtaining. Those, he tells us, are faith, hope, charity. Such qualities of character are the sole possessions which neither moth nor rust can corrupt, and which thieves cannot break through nor steal. If the Apostle's estimate of life is false, this sermon ought not to be preached. If the Apostle's words are true, to withhold it would be, in some sort, a crime.

Franklin Snow was a private Christian gentleman. He never held a public office.

The papers neither chronicled his deeds nor heralded his praises. He was neither poet, orator, scholar, nor statesman. He had not even the poor renown of wealth. No institution, endowed by him, perpetuates his name. He was a plain business man. If the success of a business man can be measured by the amount of property he accumulates, his career cannot be called successful. When he died, a few brief paragraphs in the newspapers announced that a citizen of rare energy and worth had passed away.

Why, then, should I disturb the silence that rests upon his memory? He would not have wished to be spoken of in this public way. He desired no memorial, save that which he has written in hearts that love him. He shunned notoriety. Though his voice was so often heard in prayer-meeting, who can remember ever hearing him speak of himself? Christ, duty, the Christian's joys, the Christian's privileges, these themes were continually upon his lips, but his own deeds, his own experiences, never. If, while he was seen among us, he avoided mention of himself, far less does he desire it now. If we praise his virtues, he has already heard the Master say: "Well done!" If we criticise his imperfections, he himself has learned to judge them by the standard which convicts the angels of folly. To him our best praises seem paltry now, our keenest censures superficial.

But his life teaches a lesson we can ill afford to lose. If I should tell you the story of some dazzling genius, the recital would help you only in so far as a generous admiration always purifies the breast that feels it. We admire such careers; we cannot imitate them. But achievements greater and far more to be desired than those which genius only can accomplish are possible to all of us. The best things God has put within the reach of every man. It is only the inferior things, the things for which God's immortal children cannot afford to be anxious, the things which we soon shall prize as we already prize the toys of our childhood; it is only these which any man need forego. We cannot all have health and wealth and length of days, but we all may earn faith and hope and love.

I do not point you to Franklin Snow for guidance in laying up what the world calls treasures, but in winning those possessions which God has placed us here to gain.

Therefore, I shall put slight emphasis upon his business abilities, great as they confessedly were, and shall dwell upon those successes which he won with weapons offered to us all by the Master when He said: "Thou shalt love the Lord thy God with all thy heart and thy neighbor as thyself."

By the Apostle's standard, was Mr. Snow's life a successful one?

To that question this seems the sufficient answer. Five weeks ago many of you attended his funeral in this place. It was the busiest hour of a business day. The snow and sleet were falling fast. The keen March wind blew savagely. Yet more than fifteen hundred men and women left their business, or their homes, and braved the fierce storm to come hither. While the vast congregation waited, the silence was so deep, so tender, that one who closed his eyes might think the building empty. When opportunity was given to look upon his face, all came forward. For nearly two hours the slow procession moved. Every moment of the time the air around his bier quivered with sobs. Men whom Mr. Snow's most intimate friends had never seen before paused, bent over the still face, kissed the cold forehead, and wept aloud.

Who were these mourners? You saw them, and, therefore, know I do not exaggerate their woe. One was a colored man, born and bred in slavery. " When I escaped from Richmond, he fed me and clothed me. He has been my father ever since!" One was a woman infirm with age: " When I was intemperate and sold liquor years and years ago he saved me, and taught me to love Jesus." One was a young man universally respected now: " When I had flung away my manhood, and could find no other friend to help me, he raised me from the mire, and made me all I am. He was as Christ to me." Such were some of the exclamations by which one and another of those who stood by weeping held up to view the garments which Dorcas had made.

Among these mourners came the men he had employed in business. Many of them were of different nationalities, of different religious faiths from his. They were men unused to tears. But as they passed they clasped his hand, many of them kissed his face and wept as women weep. The man who has been for twelve years foreman in his business household, when led away almost by force, broke forth in loud and bitter cries that still ring in your memory. And when the rest were gone, an old man lingered by the bier as if he could not go. In his desolate face was written the woe he uttered: "I have been in his employ at times for five and twenty years. I have lost parents and children and wife. I thought I knew trouble, but I never felt all alone before."

I have been a pastor eighteen years. I have attended many funerals, but I have never before seen the face of the dead kissed except by the lips of kinsmen. But here a multitude of men, who had never sat at his table, nor crossed the threshold of his home, were moved by an impulse that seemed irresistible to touch the dead face as Mary touched the living feet.

If you would understand a man's true character, go to his place of business: ask the men he has employed, the men to whom he has given orders, paid wages; the men who have worked for him and watched him while they worked; ask what they think of him, — ask when self-interest can no longer dictate their replies. If tears choke their voices when they try to tell you, mark that man, for there is something in him worth your minding.

Society may be deceived in him; the church may mistake long prayers for piety; self-love may cherish wife and children tenderly; but a man's servitors learn to know him as he is.

I will not pause to speak of letters which have come from far and near since that day, breathing the same sentiments which were manifested here, — letters some of them in which the writers attributed to him their own resurrection from sin into Christian manhood. For a greater triumph than Cæsar ever won that funeral procession seemed to me.

In thirty-three years a generation passes. If of those whom he had in fifty years taught to love him so many remained in this world to mourn because he had left it, how vast must be the number of those who were waiting on the other side to rejoice at his coming? To say: "We were hungry and he fed us, in prison and he visited us!"

Had he left millions of money and an intellectual renown like Webster's, these would have appeared paltry in comparison with what he carried with him to us who believe that love is the best possession. Therefore it seems worth our while to inquire why this man was so beloved! How he made himself, as it were, a part of other men's lives! In what nursery the fruit he bore was ripened.

Franklin Snow was the second of seven children. He was born at Orleans, Mass., fifty-one years ago the second of last March.[1] His parents were devout. They were not wealthy, but the business of the father, a merchant, supported the family in comfort. Franklin had not fairly learned to walk when a serious illness deprived him for life of the sight of one eye. Before he was twelve years old his four sisters died. He was but twelve when he saw the form of his father laid in the church-yard beside the forms of his sisters. Then it became necessary for the boy to leave the village school, and for his brother Gideon, three years older than himself, to go to sea. At fourteen Franklin went to Provincetown alone, and there found employment among strangers. In less than a year he was brought back to Orleans prostrated by typhus fever. His life was for a time despaired of. He awakened from delirium to learn that both his mother and his elder brother had taken the fever, and that their forms also lay in the church-yard.

[1] Spoken April, 1880.

Father, mother, four sisters, elder brother, all had been taken. There was left to him, of all his family, but one, a brother seven years old.

How cruel God often appears until time reveals his purposes! Why should this boy, gifted with a nature so affectionate, be so fearfully bereaved? Why should he be enfeebled by sickness at the crisis when he most needed strength? Why should he be forced to go forth alone, among the dangers and hardships of the world, to fight the battle of life, not only for himself, but for the child brother towards whom he felt thenceforth a father's love and a father's care? Such questions tempt one to doubt God's thought for orphans. But time often brings the answers to them.

Here in this city of Boston is an institution called "The Home for Little Wanderers." In it thousands of orphans have found help and hope and happiness. It is among the most Christlike institutions of our city. Its existence and its success are largely if not mainly due to the labors, the sacrifices, and the prayers of Mr. Snow. His hands were among the first to found it. To his last day he carried it in his heart of hearts. In the soul of the boy of fifteen, while he looked upon his own orphan brother, God wrote with the diamond-point of pain answers to the cries of many thousand orphans. So was the Captain of our Salvation made perfect by suffering. It is sufficient for the disciple to be as his Master.

Keenly as he felt his bereavements the boy uttered no complaint, but turned sturdily to his work. As soon as he had recovered sufficient strength to go he returned to Provincetown. In three years he achieved a position of responsibility and influence there. But success did not blind him to his lack of education. The nature of his occupation permitted him to be absent from it during the winter, and careful economy enabled him to spend two terms of four months each in Phillips Academy at Andover.

He studied as he had worked, with all his might. Before the close of his first term his teachers advised him to prepare for a professional life.

At Andover in his seventeenth year he deliberately gave himself to the service of Christ. There was at the time no special religious interest in the Academy. Some student, seeking assistants for the conduct of the weekly prayer-meeting, asked if he were a Christian. The question arrested his attention. He could not answer it. He retired to his room, locked the door, and resolved that he would not open it until he had answered the question. Then life opened to his thought as it had never done before. The narrow and the broad ways seemed to meet at the door of his little dormitory. When he opened it he must start forward upon one of them. Which should he choose? He thought of his family in heaven. He thought of the child brother intrusted him to lead there. He reviewed his own career until the hand which had guided and protected him seemed almost visible. With a great joy of gratitude he grasped it consciously. On his knees he gave himself to God; then arose and went forth to tell the boy who had asked him if he were a Christian that he would try to help in the prayer-meetings.

He threw himself into religious activities with the same energy which had given him success in business and in study.

He began at once to work in the prayer-meeting and in the Sunday-school. Each Sunday he walked four miles to instruct a handful of children in a neglected district. Friends felt it wise to warn him against the exhaustion that might come of excessive zeal. He answered : "I find it brings great good to myself to be thus engaged in religious work, and that I need to attend on all the means of grace."

He resolved, as one way of obeying the Master's last command, to speak in prayer-meeting whenever opportunity was offered. But he did not expect to speak without preparation. "One may pump forever," he wrote, "and get no water out of a well that is dry." He began to read the Bible carefully and prayerfully. He took notes of the sermons he heard; he wrote to Christian friends asking for facts and suggestions to be used in prayer-meetings; he searched the papers and periodicals within his reach; he sought assistance of the Seminary students and professors in furnishing his mind, until the habit was formed in him of gathering unconsciously from all directions material for devotional utterance. This was the source of his freshness in religious meetings.

With him religion was never a penance but always a delight. What many do as a price to buy heaven he did because he loved to do it. Years after leaving Andover he wrote: "It appears to me that if the Sabbath were blotted out of the privileges I enjoy, one half of all the pleasure of living would be lost."

He greatly desired to be a minister. During his second term the question was constantly in his mind. Friends and teachers advised him to gratify his wish. It cost him a hard struggle not to do so. A chief motive in his decision was that, unless he returned to business, means could not be furnished to prepare for the ministry another whom he believed by nature better fitted for it than himself.

At eighteen he came to Boston. Flattering offers had been made to detain him in Provincetown. The management of the business of the Union Wharf Company, with an ample salary, was offered him. It was a tempting prospect. But he declined it, believing that he needed a larger business experience than could be gained in a provincial town.

It is worth our while to consider what capital this boy of eighteen brought to Boston. First of all, he brought a pure soul in a pure body. Mr. Snow, his own master from his fourteenth year, was his own master. Cast at that early age into the midst of the world's temptations, without father, mother, or sister, he never experienced in any form the smirch of dissipation. Those who have known him from childhood may be safely challenged to recall one gross utterance, one indelicate expression, from his lips. He affiliated with the pure, because he was pure in heart. He never possessed that superficial polish of fine manners which is able to conceal a cancer in the soul. But in purity of manhood, in genuine delicacy and refinement of thought and feeling, he has been equalled by few and surpassed by none. His modesty was like the modesty of women in the presence of which vice cringes and is ashamed. When he gave his body to be a living sacrifice he had no infamous habits to eradicate, no pledges to sign, no infernal thirsts to fight, no festering ulcers to heal. With a magnificent physique, capable of bearing for years strains which would have crushed many a man in months, he began life's battle.

Next in the inventory of his possessions were five years of business experience patiently and laboriously acquired; habits of intense industry; the confidence and good will of all who knew him; the primary education of a village school; the results of eight months well used at Andover; the love of God supreme in his heart, and the necessity of earning each meal before he ate it. A finer capital who could ask? He sought employment at the leading fish-house in the city, and was told that, though no new help was needed, he might begin work on probation at $250 a year.

He had come from a position of authority and dignity, which he had been pressed to resume with increased emoluments. It was open to him still. But without hesitation he accepted the new position, which appears to have been offered with the expectation that he would decline it. "I hope," he wrote to his only confidential friend, "I hope I shall not have to ascend all the steps of clerkship as I have done, for that would seem pretty hard. My employment thus far has been principally to collect bills, to do some writing, to take care of the store, and when we have to deliver goods, I have to see to the marking. It is a place in which a great deal of business is done, and I think it an excellent one for a young man wishing to learn correct business habits." Brave, bright words!

It was not long before his employers found that they needed him; found that they could not afford to dispense with him. He made all their interests his own. Each morning found him the first at the wharf, and the evenings saw him the last to leave it. A few months excepted, he remained with this house until he began business in his own name. By six years of faithful service he won such consideration in the house that, when the firm dissolved, each of the partners solicited his partnership in a new firm, and when that was declined, each offered him the capital required to establish him independently in business. The offer of one was accepted, and in 1853 the name of Franklin Snow appeared at the head of a firm, which in due time took front rank among the leading fish-houses of the United States.

He had turned from the pulpit to the counting-room in obedience not to his desires, but to his sense of duty. He meant to serve God in his business. It was his conviction that all success depends upon the divine favor. Such errors as he made were errors of judgment. His exuberant hopefulness at times hurried him into complications which all his vast energy was not able to unwind. Even in questions of right and wrong his judgments were not infallible. Are any man's? But what he thought right he did. What he thought wrong he would not do. He abhorred deceit. He spoke the truth, even to his own hurt. God was in all his thoughts.

He realized how easily the flame of devotion may be extinguished by the whirlwinds of the market. "I find myself in such a continued whirlpool of business," he wrote more than twenty years ago, "that sometimes it seems I almost lose sight of that great light which came into the world to guide fallen men, but I hope by God's assistance to steer safely through the shoals and quicksands of this life. I cannot be too thankful that I gave my heart to God at the time I did, as now I fear I would not be able. It is true that we are all after the glittering gold which this world gives, but I think my thoughts are much on Christ and his glory."

When Mr. Snow came to Boston he began business in two places, — the wharf and the church. He worked in each with equal energy. He united at once with Salem Street Church. He joined the choir, led the music, paid generously towards the expenses of the society, became one of the most active tract distributers. The pastor leaned on him as on a pillar. He was rarely absent from the prayer-meeting. He was chosen deacon. He was elected superintendent of the Sunday-school.

Though never a wealthy man, his liberality was great and increasingly great to the end of his life. In one of those early years he gave to benevolent operations half of all he possessed, in addition to those generous contributions for the support of his own church, which he counted the first items of his necessary personal expenses, and paid out of his meagre salary. Accident has brought this fact to my knowledge. It is a fair type of his bountiful benevolence. The sum of his benefactions is known only in heaven, for in these matters his left hand was not the confidant of his right. He counted himself a steward of God. Yet why should I dwell on this? When a man has truly given himself to God, his money will always follow his heart. Mr. Snow gave money for others as pleasure-seekers spend money upon themselves.

I cannot discover that he ever sought or felt the need of recreations other than the joy he found in worshipping God and serving his fellow-men. But the recreations of others, especially of the young, he encouraged with energetic sympathy. He never travelled except on business; he rarely attended places of amusement, and never unless by going he could contribute to another's pleasure. The rest which most of us seek in amusements he seemed to find in prayer and praise, singing and making melody in his heart. The joy of the Lord was his strength. Many have been surprised at the facility with which he turned from the cares of business to the comforts of prayer. He would work to the last moment in his counting-room with energy the most intense, then hasten across the street, enter a prayer-meeting, usually a little late, and speak or pray as if he had come directly from hours of uninterrupted meditation. The secret of this power is an open one. He never learned the distinction between religious and secular life. He did not believe that God was farther off on Monday than on Sunday, or that He observed more carefully the way in which deacons distribute bread and wine at the communion than the way in which they distribute quintals of fish on week days.

The horizon of his charity was not bounded by the walls of his own church. I have said he was one of the founders of The Home for Little Wanderers. To the time of his death he continued one of its directors and most efficient sustainers. The Washingtonian Home, The Seaman's Friend Society, The Homœopathic School of Medicine are largely indebted to him for the good they have accomplished. He was early interested in foreign missions, and became a generous supporter of the American Board. Since his death I have learned of five strong churches which think they owe their lives to the timely aid he gave them unasked in the hours of their weakness and their need. It becomes us to remember that evening long ago when a business meeting had convened in the rooms beneath to lay a new mortgage upon the property already heavily burdened. Mr. Snow was present. He belonged to another church, and was carrying a large share of its expenses. But when he saw the trouble here his cheery voice rang out:

"Why not *pay* the floating debt!" He subscribed a third of the entire sum required, the remainder was raised at once, and the gloom of the meeting was scattered by a hopeful dawn.

Again let us not forget that when two years ago it was proposed to make that effort which has relieved our church from debt, — so that for the first time in its history its members can at last say "We owe no man anything but to love one another," — when even the pastor believed the effort greater than we ought to attempt, it was the enthusiasm and energy of Mr. Snow which mastered our hesitation and inaugurated our success.

More precious and more influential than his gifts of money were his gifts of time and thought for others. When he had become one of the prominent business men of Boston; in his own branch, I am told, the most widely known and the leading dealer in the land; directing branch houses in different cities; having established and still controlling a line of steamers to the Provinces; a bank director; carrying the work of his church almost as largely as its pastor; an active member of the Boards of

The Little Wanderers' Home, The Washingtonian Home, The Seaman's Friend Society; sustaining near his place of business a daily prayer-meeting, from which he was never absent at noon each day, this man still finds time to listen whenever suffering whispers in his presence, to go wherever prospect appears of saving a soul from sin. When his employees meet him for half an hour of prayer, they come feeling that their employer is their brother; they return to their work feeling that their brother is their employer. But they do not know that in the little memorandum book he always carries with him many of their names are written with a word or two that indicates their needs, and guides him as he plans for their spiritual health and remembers them in his secret prayers.

But, friends, it is not what we do but what we are that creates our influence and decides our destiny. Our deeds are only chisels with which our characters are sculptured. I have given this outline of biography to indicate the school in which the man we mourn was formed. It was not what he did but what he was that made Franklin Snow so well beloved.

You have resolved to place his portrait in your prayer-room. There it will say to all who knew him, with an emphasis not possible to naked words, FAITH, HOPE, CHARITY; BUT THE GREATEST OF THESE IS CHARITY. His faith was great, his hope was great. Both were in him the children of Charity.

1. Men loved him because he loved men. You know how his great heart beat toward you, his associates in this church. But he could also feel for those with whose ways he could not sympathize. To the drunkard this most temperate of men was a brother. To the profligate this pure man was a stern but tender friend. For the penurious this generous giver had never a word of criticism. In transgressors he saw brothers to be helped. The sins of men grieved but did not easily provoke him. His mission was not to censure but to save.

He was long-suffering with the fallen. Again and again he has lifted the same man from the same mire, still hoping all things. He taught the despairing to hope for themselves because he still hoped for them.

After years of intimacy I cannot recall a word spoken by him of the absent which he would not have spoken in their presence.

When he could not praise he was silent. But when his official duty in the church compelled him to recognize evil in others and describe it, he painted the guilty as the Greek artist painted Alexander, — the monarch's hand covering the scar upon his brow, — that so he might follow charity in loyalty to truth.

He was quick to sympathize with the joys of others, for next to making men good he delighted in making them happy.

Born on that sandy stretch of land which, coveting no luxury of flowers or of fruits, thrusts its brave breast far forth into the Atlantic, meets the cold north currents, turns them from Rhode Island and Connecticut, and gives to those states the mild and genial climate it seeks not for itself, his birthplace typifies himself. Early taught by stern necessity to live for another, years confirmed in him that love which seeketh not her own.

2. Hope! He was its harbinger, its incarnation. He radiated joy as the sun sheds light. He seemed the gladdest man I ever knew. He was born with a buoyant temperament. But natural spirits alone cannot sustain such joyousness as his beneath such

burdens as he bore. The chirrup of the cricket ceases when the fire is extinguished. They only can sing always who have learned the song of Moses and the Lamb. Men who forget that through much tribulation we must enter the kingdom may be surprised to know the school in which his gladness grew. If the expression did not belong to the high and holy One, we might be tempted while we consider the early life of our friend to call him "a man of sorrows," and to marvel that he least of all could be called a sorrowful man. His later life was not remote from grief. Three of his children he followed to the grave. After years of incessant toil he was compelled to endure in his business experience a mortification and anguish whose poignancy God only knew. He carried it so nobly that strangers scarcely suspected it was in him. The shock of it was the initial cause of his death. He carried that sorrow to his grave. For years he has been an overworked, a tired man. His health had been so impaired that animal spirits were replaced by physical depression. Yet still the bright face beamed hope and cheer among us. Still strangers visiting our church inquired who it was that "furnished sunshine for that aisle." His face drove away despondency. It made us ashamed to moan. When others pointed to the shadow, he pointed to the sun that cast it. When others said, "We fear the thunder in the cloud," he said, "The cloud is his chariot." His presence in the prayer-meeting was as the coming of a spring breeze to refresh others less weary than himself. In his death it seems not so much as if a star had been taken from our sky, but rather as if some strange eclipse was shedding gloom from horizon to horizon.

And this was more than a sunny temperament. It came of discipline and prayer. He schooled himself to carry his sorrows alone, and to share his joys with all. So the fine furnace receives the black coals into its heart, and gives them back to others transmuted into radiance and warmth. There is no quality of manhood rarer than this. To say, while bearing the cross, "My joy I give unto you." This is the offspring of that love which seeketh not her own, which, when it fasts, disfigures not the countenance, but anoints the head and washes the face, and appears not unto men to fast, but unto the Father which seeth in secret.

3. His faith came of obedience working by love. His trust in God was of the unconscious sort which children have toward their parents. It was not gained by reasoning, and by reasoning it could not be displaced. By doing the will of God he came to know the truth of Christ. He was not conscious of that religious uncertainty which permeates the air. Sermons to Thomas seemed to him a waste of time. Eternal verities were realities to him. He could not argue in defence of them, for that would imply a possibility of their being false. But when one's spirit was tormented with doubts of that which to doubt is a living death, — doubts which learned doctors cannot cure,— his presence and his prayers would often banish them as sunlight drives away the dismal creatures that infest the night.

As one who, laboring with gauze and velvet and knife and needle, makes at last an artificial flower, fastens the poor thing on her bosom, and goes forth proud of her ornament; but when she sees by the wayside a violet which has grown, no one knows how, by simply looking at the sun, receiving the dew of heaven, and letting its heart dilate as the spirit of beauty inspires, the lady casts aside her artificial gaud, and clasps the genuine flower; so I turn from the reasonings of the schools to the grand child-like faith of this inerudite disciple; faith which grew strong in the world's highway through simply loving the Lord Jesus and doing his commandments, — and know that my Redeemer liveth.

When our hearts are heavy and our way grows dark, when we are tempted to fear that God has forgotten us, let us remember the orphan child, enfeebled by sickness, leaving his ruined home. Let us follow him in our thought through six and thirty years of trials, struggles, victories, defeats, till we see the great multitude weeping around his bier. Let us think of the life he is living now, and return to our appointed work reassured that the hairs of our heads also are numbered by One who is with us always even unto the end of the world.

XIII.

WHAT MUST I DO TO BE SAVED?

Sirs, what must I do to be saved? — ACTS xvi. 30.

THIS is a question often asked, and rarely answered. Every good resolution formed, every evil habit combated, evinces a soul asking what it must do to be saved. At times the quest grows eager. The man is burdened with the weight of his immortality. Unrest deepens into anguish. Silent questionings become outcries. He turns to those in whom he confides, — the men on whom he recognizes the livery of the Great King, — saying, "Sirs, what must I do to be saved?"

The question was asked by many persons, in varied and dissimilar circumstances, of the inspired teachers. By them, I think, it was never answered twice in precisely the same terms. If each of us should ask the question of many religious teachers, it is probable that we would all receive nearly the same reply; we would be answered in one of two or three stereotyped phrases, — we would be told to "believe in the Lord Jesus Christ," or to " give our hearts to Jesus," or " to love Jesus."

I will endeavor to remind you, first, how the Master and his Apostles answered the question, and then to compare our answers with theirs.

1. As far as the New Testament shows, when any man inquired what he should do to be saved, the inspired teachers pointed him to some one definite, intelligible act. It was generally something he was least inclined to do. It was always something he could not possibly misunderstand. We will commence at the beginning.

John the Baptist came preaching in the wilderness of Judæa, and saying, " Repent ye, for the kingdom of heaven is at hand." Many hearts were stirred by religious feeling. Multitudes came to the preacher, asking what they should do. Their fears and their hopes had been excited. They felt the need of more instruction. " What do you mean by telling us to repent? We want to repent. Tell us how. What shall we do?"

To each the prophet returned a swift, clear-cut, piercing reply, — such a reply that the seeker could not remain in doubt what he ought to do next; could not remain an instant groping for the door, as a man gropes in the dark.

We have reports of four interviews with four different classes of inquirers.

First. The Pharisees and Sadducees came to him. They represented the religious classes; they filled that place among the contemporaries of John which professing Christians, church-members, occupy among us. Some of them were good men. Some of them were bad men. All supposed themselves special favorites of Heaven, because they were lineal descendants of Abraham. God had covenanted, long before, to remember the seed of Abraham forever. On that promise they grounded their hopes. When these men asked, "What shall we do?" John said to them, "Stop saying to yourselves we have Abraham to our father; for God is able of these stones to raise up children unto Abraham. Judge yourselves by the same standards you apply to other men. A wicked Pharisee is not better off than a wicked publican, but worse; for he sins against more light. If you are good men, and bear good fruit, well; if you are bad men, and bear bad fruit, the axe is laid at your roots; ye shall be hewn down, and cast into the fire."

From the New Testament we have fabricated a theory the fac-simile of that which the Pharisees constructed from the Old. We have abused Paul's doctrine of the perseverance of the saints, into a notion that men who have passed through a certain gamut of emotions will be saved, whether they become saints or continue sinners. This notion, utterly without scriptural warrant, tinges our thinking, and twists our practice. Translated into the language of to-day, John's words are addressed to us, members of churches, and they are these: " Think not to say within yourselves, we have been converted, we are safe; for I say unto you, God is able out of those wooden pews to raise up converted men. The axe is laid at your roots. Every one of you that beareth not fruit shall be hewn down, and cast into the fire." All spiritual children of Abraham bear fruit. The promises are for them alone. All truly converted persons become good; not perfect in a moment,— there are unlovely Christians,— but better than they were before they were converted.

There must be a change in fact, not in fancy.

Second. The common people came, asking, "What shall we do?" The answer was equally precise: "Let him that hath two coats give to him that hath none; and he that hath meat, let him do likewise."

The masses are poor. Poverty tends to make men penurious. The drudgery of incessant toil, with small returns, tends to render them over-careful. One who has inherited wealth, or won it by speculation, is prone to prodigality. But when a competence is obtained cent by cent, saving here and grinding there, the tendency is to hardness. Money being the one thing toiled for, and saved for, and lived for, assumes an undue value in the possessor's eyes: it is hard for him to give it away. Despite the splendid exceptions, which gleam in the lives of the poor like diamonds set in black, poverty is prone to make men thoughtless of others, over-careful for themselves. To this class of men, asking what they should do, John replied, " Give, give, give."

Third. The publicans asked, "What shall we do?" These were the tax-gatherers. It was more difficult for them to defraud their government than it is for our revenue collectors; but it was much easier for them to levy blackmail upon the people. They could not reach up and take from the Roman eagle's nest; his eyes were too keen, his talons too sharp: but they could reach down into the people's pockets, and take what they would.

There was no power to prevent the publican from visiting any merchant and demanding a talent. If asked the reason of the tax, the reply was at hand, "Because, if you do not hand over *one*, I will have you fined two!" The merchant must choose between bribery and ruin. If he refused the claim, the wealth of government would be used against him. It cost the publican nothing to go to law: government paid *his* costs. But it would be costly for the private individual, and he was sure of losing his case. This was the reason why the people so thoroughly detested the publicans. Doubtless there were honest tax-gatherers besides Zaccheus and Levi; but history has not preserved their names. The taint of their class was upon all. They could not be respected. They must be rich, or ciphers. The government's enormous demands allowed no margin for legitimate profits. They could not gain wealth by fair means. The temptation to gain it by foul means was superlative.

To the publicans John said simply, "Exact no more than is appointed you." Translated into the language of to-day, his words are to every whiskey inspector, bank examiner, custom-house officer, revenue collector, government employee from the chief magistrate down to the municipal policeman, who would save his soul, "Take nothing more than your salary." If this command were obeyed, the machinery of government might stop, but the wheels of God's kingdom might advance more swiftly than they do.

Fourth. The soldiers came, asking, "What shall we do?" The special sins of those soldiers were three. Familiarity with bloodshed had brutalized them. Further, they were in a subjugated country. Sedition was punishable not only by death, but by confiscation of the convict's property. Part of the confiscated wealth fell to the executioners. The soldiers were the executioners. They were therefore strongly tempted to accuse innocent persons in order to obtain their wealth. Again: the stated pay, even of Roman soldiers, was small.

Booty and glory were the expected compensations. In small and conquered provinces, like Syria, there was no prospect of glory or of booty. Hence the temptation to mutinous discontent was strong, because the voyage was monotonous, and the hope of prize-money small.

To those soldiers John said, —

"Do no violence."

"Accuse no man falsely."

And, hardest of all, —

"Be content with your wages."

These are the only recorded conversations of John with inquirers. He gave each something definite to do. It was, in each case, the thing the seeker was least likely and least willing to do. John allowed no one to remain a moment in doubt. He encouraged none to spend ten seconds examining the quality of their emotions. Whether they felt well, or ill, or indifferently, he treated as a matter altogether immaterial. If they began to be better men than they had been, that was evidence of their repentance; if they were *not* better men, — no matter what they felt or hoped or feared, — they had not repented. He said to each one, "Stop doing the wrong you have been doing; begin the right you have been neglecting:" and he showed each what that meant for *him*.

We pass on to the Master's instruction to inquirers. To the young man asking what he should do to inherit eternal life, Jesus replied, "Keep the commandments." This the young man claimed to have done. "What more shall I do?" — "Sell all thou hast, and give to the poor," replied the Lord. When men impressed by the Master's miracles came to him, he assigned them duties equally definite. He bade some leave their friends, even their unburied fathers, and endure the hardship of following Him who had not where to lay his head; or he directed others to forego the luxury of his presence, return to their own friends, and face the odium of being called disciples of the Nazarene.

He laid no emphasis upon emotions, but endeavored to make the inquirer's emotions the steam to drive his conduct. He warned men not to base their confidence upon their feelings. When Peter was sure of himself, because he felt full of love, Jesus warned him of the approaching fall. When surrounded by crowds of enthusiastic and admiring hearers, he would not trust himself to them, because he knew what was in men, but departed secretly out of their midst. When the whole city approached him, waving branches, and shouting "Hosanna in the highest," his eyes were wet with tears, while he cried, "O Jerusalem, Jerusalem! that stonest the prophets."

Paul's example travels the same path. He abounds in lists of vices and virtues. He reiterates, that if men's emotions lead them to perform the virtues and avoid the vices, they have evidence that they are converted. Emotions which do not work this result are delusive. Sorrow itself in the sinner may be a sign of good or of evil. The only proof that it is not a sorrow itself needing to be repented of, is, that it works certain practical results.

The New Testament seeks in men's conduct the evidence of their conversion. We almost never seek it there.

2. Our answers to inquirers are generally vague. When a man under religious excitement asks us what he shall do, we rarely tell him anything definite, — anything he can understand. If the most penurious man we know asked what he should do to be saved,

we should not dare to tell him, "Give a hundred thousand dollars to the poor;" yet we all should feel that his religion would be a sham until it touched his pockets.

Afraid to tell men they must do right if they would be saved, we take refuge in certain scriptural phrases, which were once full of meaning, but which are empty cups as we offer them.

First. We tell men "to repent." Suppose they ask us what we mean. We do not mean "feel distressed." The man *is* distressed; we want to relieve him. We dare not say, feel happy; there may be no ground in him for rejoicing.

The Apostles would not have delayed an instant over the man's feelings. They would have discovered his besetting sin, or his nearest neglected duty, and directed him to that. If penurious, they would have told him to give to the poor. If he were a coward, they would have told him that he must be born, not only of the Spirit, but of water; that is, baptized, — wear publicly in daylight the badge of the new and despised calling, instead of seeking Jesus by night, for fear of the Jews.

This would be the result. Either the inquirer would obey, and gain strength of character, — become a better man, — or he would go away sorrowful, *knowing* that he was not a Christian. There would be no possibility of self-delusion; no possibility of his settling down, with heart unchanged, into a deadly lethargy of church-membership, until startled by the revealing voice, "I never knew you!"

Second. Another cloud in which we take refuge is this: "Give yourself to Jesus." The phrase is hallowed by so long a usage, that we suppose it quite intelligible. Doubtless, when first employed, the phrase was terse and clear; but it has risen like a fog, to hide the gate of God from many an inquirer. "You tell me to give myself to Jesus:" I want to; but how can I? You have been urging me to do a definite act; but when I ask you what I am to do, you sing to me, —

"Nothing either great or small remains for me to do."

Now the expression, "Give yourself to Jesus," means exactly this: obey Jesus. When we say a man is giving himself to drink, we mean he gets drunk. Giving one's self to study means studying. To give one's self to fashion, means to obey fashion. Giving one's self to Garibaldi, means obeying Garibaldi. To give yourself to Jesus, means to obey Jesus, — to begin doing instantly, without reference to your inward sensations, the thing Jesus has commanded; probably a different thing in the case of each one of you.

If you are angry, it means, "First, go and be reconciled to thy brother, and then come and offer thy gift." If, like Peter, you are afraid of an unbelieving world, it means, "Go feed my sheep, and dare to be crucified for it with your head downward, if need be."

Third. We often bewilder men by telling them to "Believe in the Lord Jesus Christ." The inquirer replies, "I do believe that Jesus is the Christ; I always have believed: it is impossible for me to believe more than I do."

When the Apostles employed that expression, it carried a definite and exact idea. It meant what giving one's self to Christ means, — it meant obeying Christ.

Here is a sick man, and he has no hope of recovery. You tell him, if he only believed in your doctor, he would get well.

You do not mean that any change of opinion, or any new intellectual appreciation in itself, will cure him; but that taking your doctor for his doctor, swallowing his medicines, obeying his directions, will bring health.

Believe, and be baptized, said Paul to the jailer. Till then, the jailer was one of the pagans. For him to submit to baptism was to take the first prescription; it was to break with his old and degrading associates and associations, to take the first step among new and redeeming company. It was to take Jesus for his Lord and Saviour.

3. I have said that, if we imitate the Master, we will help the inquirer to perceive his nearest neglected duty, and urge him to seek evidence of his conversion in the faithful performance of that.

This we rarely do. If any man has been, though ever so long ago, under certain religious impressions, — if he has felt first distressed and afterwards delighted, — we receive this as the most satisfactory evidence of conversion. Unless he has subsequently been flagrantly immoral, no examining committee questions his evidences; least of all does he doubt them himself. I can find no warrant for this in the Bible. Paul did not base his hopes on the visions he had seen, but labored lest, while saving others, he should himself become a castaway. There was nothing in Peter's past that ought to have dried denying Peter's tears.

By this, John knew that he had passed from death unto life: not because a divine voice had called him from the nets; not because he had lain upon the Saviour's bosom; not because his heart had glowed with rapture of apocalyptic vision; not because he had been called the disciple whom Jesus loved; not because he had loved the brethren, and for their sakes endured tribulation; not because he had been persecuted for the faith, — but because *then*, at the time of writing, he obeyed Christ by loving the brethren. Another might have had all his past experiences; but if such a man said he loved God, while hating his brother, he would be a liar, and the truth not in him.

Paul, Peter, John, would no more have based their hopes upon some past sensations than you would think of dining to-day on the memory of the milk you drank in infancy. The result of our vague and often deluding replies to inquirers is seen in the condition of Christian communities. Men have not been trained to seek evidence of conversion in performance of duties, but in experience of prescribed sensations. There are men and women not a few, in the churches, who will never draw nearer heaven until some influence sweeps away their "evidences." They trust in them, not in Christ. How often do we hear men say, "I am sure I am a Christian, because I once felt thus and so." If Jesus Christ were dead, it would be equally true that they once experienced those feelings. They are like the enchanted sleepers, nodding before the magician's lyre. If conscience pricks, they find balm in their "evidences." They neither watch nor pray; they enter freely into temptation; they do not love the Master's work; they do not feed the hungry, nor clothe the naked, nor visit the sick and in prison: they do worship mammon; they do love the chief seats in the synagogues, and to be called of men Rabbi! When God rains conviction, they make a stout umbrella of their "evidences," and not a drop touches them.

Beside these self-satisfied ones, who think the work was all completed long ago, sit others of a different temper, — men prayerful, men with a sorrowful sense of sin, men struggling against temptation. They have a deep appreciation of Jesus' character. They strive to imitate and obey Him. Daily they climb upwards. But they do not count themselves Christians; others do not count them Christians. Sleek Pharisees lament over them as "sinners," because they have had no such emotional experience as dead professors delight in.

These men I count as the most hopeful candidates for heaven. They are spared the peril of relying upon past evidences, and they shall have the sweet surprise of those who say, "Lord, when saw we thee in prison, and visited thee?"

The first class are like those prairie-trees that glowed an hour in glorious flame, when the fire swept the plain, and ever since have stood dead, charred trunks. The other class are like the hidden germs, warmed by the same heat, which grew unseen, and made the harvest.

XIV.

WHAT HAS GOD DONE TO SAVE ME?

> And there cometh to him a leper beseeching him, and kneeling down to him, and saying unto him, If thou wilt, thou canst make me clean. And being moved with compassion, he stretched forth his hand and touched him, and saith unto him, I will, be thou clean. And straightway the leprosy departed from him, and he was made clean. — MARK i. 40-43. (R. V.)

THE text leads us to consider a momentous theme, the salvation of our souls. But what I have to say will not be worth your minding, unless we can keep steadily in mind three facts, which, though they are familiar and certain, are often overlooked precisely when they should fill the horizon of our thoughts. The facts are these : —

I. Jesus Christ is the same yesterday, to-day, and forever.

II. He who hath seen Him hath seen the Father.

III. In the New Testament the same word is, when used to describe Christ's treatment of sick bodies, translated, " make whole," that is, "restore to health," but, when employed to describe Christ's treatment of sinful souls, is rendered "save," whatever that may mean.

For example: In the account of the cure of the issue of blood, the word occurs three times. The woman thought, "If I may but touch his garment I shall *be made whole.*" The Master said, "Daughter, be of good comfort; thy faith hath *made thee whole.*" The evangelist adds, she "was *made perfectly whole.*"

But the same word is rendered, "They shall call his name Jesus, because He shall *save* his people from their sins;" "The Son of Man is come to seek and to *save* that which was lost."

By using two distinct English words, which are not synonyms, to render the same original, a fact which Christ taught with careful emphasis has been obscured; namely, that his healing men's bodies illustrated and revealed what He came into the world to do for our souls. He compared himself to a physician, not because he ministered unto the body, but to the spirit. It was not of invalids, but of robust publicans and sinners, that he said, "They that are whole have no need of a physician, but they that are sick. I am come not to call the righteous, but sinners to repentance." The divinely offered key, therefore, to a right appreciation of Christ's spiritual work, even to that which theologians call the Atonement, should be sought, I think, by observing how our Lord cleansed the lepers, made the blind to see, and the lame to walk. And this is, I believe, the only key which has not been employed to unlock that mystery.

Let us endeavor to realize how He, whose name is the only name given under heaven among men whereby we may be saved, healed men's diseases, in order that we may understand, so far as it has been revealed, how He saves us from our sins.

I. Consider first why Jesus healed. There came a leper to Him. The leper knelt before Him, beseeching Him and crying, "If thou wilt, thou canst make me clean."

"If thou wilt" is not a future. The verb is in the present tense and signifies volition. The words mean, "If you wish to, you can cure me."

Some exegetes infer, from a Greek word employed later in the narrative, that the leper must have entered the house where

Jesus was teaching. Others think that he came to Christ when the multitude followed him down the Mount of the Beatitudes. For a leper to do either of these things was an outrage. It was as if a man broken out with small-pox should enter a street-car or walk down that aisle. Jesus himself rebuked the man sharply, we read in the forty-third verse. But he did not rebuke until he had healed him. Remember that by coming to this place the leper had broken both the civil and ecclesiastical law; he had defied the commandments given through Moses; possibly he had endangered the health, even the lives of others; certainly he had greatly alarmed them. They were many; he was one. He had therefore done an exceedingly selfish act. Still, when the leper cried, "You can heal me if you wish to," Jesus was sorry for him. He said, "I do wish to heal you."

Then Christ healed the man, not to show that He could, but because He pitied the sufferer.

This was characteristic of all our Lord's cures. When asked to work miracles to prove his ability to do so, He habitually declined. Every act of healing wrought by Christ was an act of pure compassion.

He never healed to attract attention to himself. He often commanded those He healed to say nothing of their cure. Often, as in this instance, he sent the man he had healed instantly away out of sight. When, in spite of his wish, his miracles attracted so much attention that men's minds were by them diverted from his teachings, "He departed out of their midst," and went where He could preach to ears that were not stopped by wonder. He fed the multitudes because He had compassion upon them, seeing that they were hungry and faint and had far to go.

"Jesus Christ, the same yesterday, to-day, and forever."

"He that hath seen me hath seen the Father."

II. Consider next how Jesus healed.

1. The fact that He had compassion upon them was itself the first step in the cure of many who came to Him.

Physicians tell me there are diseases in which recovery must begin by regaining lost self-respect. The most hopeless symptom of certain maladies — generally they are those induced by dissipation — is a sense of utter degradation. It may be only the reflection of a false but intense public opinion. Strangers say, "I will waste no sympathy on him. He has only what he deserves. He ought to be ashamed of himself." Never a trace of such sentiment in Christ's treatment of any man. The most dissolute and disgraced found in Him not only pity, but a delicate considerateness which rekindled their self-respect. The demoniacs belonged to a class degraded by their own conduct, at least according to a current opinion, which may have been false, but certainly obtained. Christ began the cure of the demoniac of Gadara by treating him with the respect one gentleman shows toward another; treating him as the poor creature had not been treated since his malady began. He inquired, "What is thy name?" It was equivalent to exchanging cards in modern high society. The demoniac had cried out, "What have I to do with thee, Jesus, thou Son of the Most High God." Christ replied in effect, "You have mentioned my name: may I ask yours?"

He completed the cure by sending the man home to those who had known only to despise him, with this message, "Go tell thy friends that God hath had compassion on thee, and give them the proof. Show them what great things God hath done for thee." It was like sending to his home, decorated with orders from the sovereign, one who had left his native city a disgraced beggar.

When a man palsied by his own sins — we have the Master's authority for that — had been borne of four and laid before Him, while the Pharisees from Jerusalem regarded him with contemptuous repugnance, as thoughtless or inexperienced men often look upon a confirmed inebriate, Our Lord began that man's cure by restoring his self-respect. He said, "Thy sins are forgiven thee." That is, " God respects you."

He treated these invalids as He treated the publicans and sinners. When they " drew near for to hear Him," and the Pharisees " murmured, saying, This man receiveth sinners and eateth with them," He spoke the parable of the prodigal, which said to the outcasts, " God is glad you have come, though these religious teachers think themselves defiled by your approach."

But of all Christ's acts no other, I think, so instantaneously restored to men that lost self-respect, without which physical recovery is sometimes, and moral reformation is always, impossible, as his touching the lepers.

We can scarcely conceive what the effect must have been upon a man who had for years been closeted with his loathsome self, or with still more loathsome fellow-sufferers; a man who might not eat with human beings unless the same deadly taint was upon them, nor appear in the street except jangling a bell to give warning of the peril his presence brought; who, if he patted upon the head a carrion dog, it must be instantly killed, lest it should brush against others and defile them because he had touched it; who, if he saw his mother, his child, his wife approach must fly or shout, "Unclean, unclean, keep afar!" We can scarcely conceive what the effect must have been upon such a man, when he saw Jesus draw nigh.

The multitude attending the Saviour falls back as men shrink from the plague, for crowds are always cowards. But the Master approaches, and paying no heed to the jangling-bell, the warning cry, lays his hand upon him. For the first time in years the leper feels the touch of a hand that is not hardened by the awful malady. That touch must have made the leper a new man in heart before the quickened pulse could shoot new life into the decaying limbs.

2. But more is signified in those words: "He put forth his hand and touched him." They suggest, what other passages confirm, that in healing Christ made effort. We are accustomed to think of the Master's miracles as wrought without exertion. As if they cost Him nothing; as if He were a piece of machinery, an iron man, no more exhausted by the good He did than is an elevator which carries you aloft by steam. But Christ is not so revealed. It is written, "Himself took our infirmities, and bore our diseases;" "He hath borne our griefs, and carried our sorrows, and by his stripes are we healed."

If you have watched one suffer whose pain it was harder to behold than to endure, because you loved her more than she loved herself; if you have held your own little child in the dental chair while the great tooth was drawn, and almost rebelled against the fiat which prevented you from taking the pain you were compelled to witness, — you have a guide to the right understanding of those words. One must be blind to read the New Testament, and fancy Christ's cures cost Him nothing because He was divine. It was because He was divine that they cost Him so much. If you would seek beings incapable of suffering, you must go not up toward the angels and the great white throne, for there you will find "the Lamb as it had been slain," but down among the oysters.

Ewald, who has seen further than most into the spirit of the New Testament, reminds us that when Christ healed the dumb man, He looked up to heaven as if seeking reinforcement of strength. He looked up to heaven and sighed. When the woman was healed He felt that virtue, that is, strength, had gone from Him. He approached the grave of Lazarus groaning within himself as a man in stress. He looked up and prayed before offering the prayer which He uttered for the sake of them "that stood by." He led the blind man away from the crowd, as if seeking to be as "undisturbed as possible." He put all but the three friends and the parents out of the room when He restored to life the daughter of Jairus. He took Peter's wife's mother by the hand and "lifted her up."

Thus He bore men's diseases. He sighed, He prayed, He lifted them in his arms, He put his hands upon them, He drew them to his bosom, He groaned, He felt his strength go from Him, to heal their bodies. If He had done less He would not have made manifest the long-suffering God ; and his saving men's bodies, his bearing their infirmities and healing their diseases, would have been no illustration of the agony with which He wrestled in Gethsemane for the salvation of their souls.

"Jesus Christ, the same yesterday, to-day, and forever."

"He that hath seen me hath seen the Father," saith He who is the Saviour of the body and the Saviour of the soul.

3. Again, in many instances we are told, that Jesus employed known remedies in physical healing. He manipulated the palsied tongue and the stopped ears ; " put his fingers in the ears ; " " touched the tongue." He covered the blind eyes with moist clay, a well-known Egyptian remedy for ophthalmia. He inquired minutely the symptoms of the demoniac boy. He bent over those He healed, He touched them, as careful physicians do.

Those who came asking his help for their sick besought Him to lay his hands upon them, as if this was known to be his usual method of healing. When He sent his disciples forth in his name, they anointed the sick with oil, a common remedy, and James refers to that as still customary among those who followed their example. James v. 14 teaches the reverse of what it is often fancied to mean. It bids us use the best remedies known, and pray while we employ them, for the fervent, effectual prayer of the righteous man availeth much while he uses the right remedies, of which anointing with oil was among the commonest, and is therefore given as representative of all.

In healing the demoniac of Gadara, we are told Christ did two things which every physician experienced in the treatment of the insane would wish to have done. He began by asking the maniac his name. There was more in that than the soothing influence already noted. The question was calculated to divert the man's attention from his distracting malady. Sometimes, with the insane, to divert is to inaugurate the cure. To convince the man that he is well may be to complete his cure. Often the last step is the more difficult.

A victim of intemperance was dashing himself hither and thither at risk of life in vain attempts to elude the monstrous phan-torn serpent he saw assailing him. Nurses and physician were baffled. Opiates had no effect. The man must sleep or he must die. A new physician was summoned. He entered the room with a huge bare knife, attacked the phantom serpent, fought it, drove it under the bed, while the cowering wretch watched every motion in an agony of alternating hopes and fears; stabbed it again and again, slew it, dragged it across the floor, threw it from the door, locked the door again; and the sufferer, with a great sigh of relief, sank into a slumber which saved his reason and his life.

May not such an experience throw light upon the fact that Jesus allowed the devils to enter into the swine and drive them down a steep place into the sea, where they were choked? Certainly not until he had seen that, did the demoniac sit at the feet of Jesus " clothed and in his right mind."

Thus did Jesus encourage, not the breach but the observance of God's order. He put honor, by his example, upon the use of scientific remedies. At times he healed by a word, without approaching the sick one. But He seems to have dispensed with remedies only when to employ them was impossible, or when they would have been obviously useless, or when there was a special reason for neglecting them. His example said to those Apostles to whom miraculous powers were given, "Use the best means; pray God to bless their use; and when you can do nothing more, pray." And that is what every wise and instructed Christian strives to do.

4. But in all Christ's healings there was conspicuously revealed the authority of absolute power. In every instance the sufferer was made to feel that the secret and source of his cure lay in the fact which justified the words, "I wish it, therefore be thou clean." The presence of supernatural power was so obvious that those who would not concede the agency of God were forced to assume the ministry of Satan, and to say, " He casteth out devils by Beelzebub, the prince of the devils."

Others might pity the sufferer, might love him, grieve over him, use all known appliances, spend all their strength, to help him; the four might bear the palsied man in their arms and break open roofs to make way for him; the father might suffer many deaths, because his son cast himself now into the water and now into the fire; men might bind the demoniac with chains, and the woman might spend all that she had upon physicians, — in vain. Jesus alone could say with authority, "I will, be thou clean."

When He spoke, devils obeyed, the dead heard, the despairing hoped, the lost knew that they were found.

"The same yesterday, to-day, and forever." "He that hath seen me hath seen the Father," saith Jesus Christ, the Saviour of the body, the Saviour of the soul.

If you ask me to explain the Atonement, I cannot, though I might perhaps, as well as another, darken counsel by words without knowledge. If you ask me how God, by the sacrifice of his Son, saves men from their sins, I point you to Jesus Christ delivering men from their diseases. There we may find all we need to know, all I believe we can know, until we have grown into larger intellectual growth and loftier mental stature than in this world we shall reach. For in Jesus we see God revealed not as a king, a judge, a potentate afar off, but Immanuel, God with us, calling us, coming after us, lifting us, encouraging us, hoping for us when we cannot hope for ourselves, giving himself for us, healing our diseases, and bearing our iniquities.

XV.

THE MISSIONARY SPIRIT.

For I could wish that myself were accursed from Christ for my brethren, my kinsmen according to the flesh. — ROM. ix. 3.

THIS is the most perfect illustration known to me of Paul's own assertion that the letter killeth, but the spirit maketh alive. Measure the words with rule and compass, weigh them in mathematical scales, and they are an offence to God and man. How much sunlight have I between my two hands? Box in the space, to make sure you include no more, no less. Apply the carpenter's rule. You have no sunlight; blank darkness only. Treat the words of the text in that same way. Consider them apart from the man who wrote them, apart from the mental exaltation in which he wrote them, and you put an extinguisher upon a burning lamp.

"I could wish myself accursed from Christ for my brethren." Could St. Paul deliberately say that? Could he deliberately oppose his own desires to his Master's will, and prefer his kinsmen's welfare to his Saviour's blessing? Certainly not. But in the text does he not say he could? Certainly he does. Bring your dictionary and your grammar. They will not weave the words for you into any other meaning. With lexicons and grammars only, men have tried for eighteen hundred years to extract from the expression some saintlier significance.

But identical phrases do not always carry the same meanings.

"I want to die!" So moans Pericles of Tyre. He has lost his wife, his child, his throne. You may pity him. But pity cannot blind judgment. You know the wish is weak and wicked. It is rebellion against the Powers above.

Hear the same words on other lips. The Austrian squadrons stand firm, each one an impenetrable hedge of spears. Switzerland is lost unless those squares are broken. "I want to die!" It is the voice of Winkelried, as he gathers the spears into his bosom, breaks the squares, and saves his country. Is it right to want to die? No! Did not a hero say it? Yes! Was he not, then, weak and wicked? Go measure tape with that yardstick. It may serve to measure tape. It will not suffice to measure lightning.

The words of the text are a window in the Apostle's breast. Through them appears a great soul struggling with emotions too fervent for control. It will be our wisdom not to criticise the words, but to catch such gleams as we may of the spirit that shines through them.

This Epistle to the Romans is Paul's most splendid utterance. It contains his last appeal to his countrymen, his final plea with the Jews to become Christians. Every power of his heart and brain is strained. He begins as a lawyer addressing a jury. He is sternly logical until each proposition has been proved. In the outset he announces his theme to be "concerning Jesus Christ" our Lord. Next he proves that the Gentiles need a Saviour. Third, that the Jews must perish if they have no Redeemer. Fourth, that God has provided for both an all-sufficient Saviour in his Son. Thus far each fagot is placed with careful accuracy. Then the match is applied. The logic blazes. Flames ascend. They dart upward. They wrap the pile in fire. He enters realms of feeling where literal speech is impossible. Metaphors are thrown off like sparks from wheels which revolve too fast for sight to follow. Expressions are poured out which seem incoherent and unintelligible except to those who share the writer's exaltation.

He has proved that without Christ all men are lost, and lost hopelessly. He turns to show the abounding love of God, who in his Son has opened a way of salvation for all. He strives to express the magnitude of that salvation. Carried beyond himself, he breaks forth in the grandest of all his doxologies : " I am persuaded that neither death nor life, nor angels nor principalities nor powers, nor things present nor things to come, nor heighth nor depth, nor any other creature, shall be able to separate us from the love of God, which is in Jesus Christ our Lord."

Borne far beyond the present, his pinions bathed in light of the Eternal love, he remembers the unutterable loss of those who will not go with him. Must he leave his people in their darkness? The thought wrings his heart. A counter-wave of horror rushes over him. It sweeps him from Hermon into Gethsemane. Never perhaps before has he approached so near the mind of Him who wept over his countrymen, crying, "O Jerusalem, how often would I have gathered thy children, and ye would not."

His father, his mother, — great Israel, with all its faults the noblest race the earth has seen; to whom first the promises were given, first the glory was offered; stem of which Christ himself had come! — these Israelites alone of all the world he sees rejecting the world's Saviour. The Master's own parable is in his brain. The great day is near, has come. He sees the chosen people, his own people, upon the left hand. He hears the words, "Depart from me, ye accursed!" That he sees, that he hears. For the instant he sees no more, hears no more. He cannot reason, he can only feel. "My brethren are doomed! My brethren are lost!" Love shrieks while reason reels: "Save them! Send me away, but save them! I am one, they are many." In such a moment come the words: "I could wish myself accursed from Christ for my brethren, whose are the fathers, from whom as concerning the flesh Christ came, who is over all, God blessed for ever. Amen."

After that "Amen," I think, Paul's pen stopped; stopped long enough for emotion to vent itself in tears. The next sentence reveals a serener mood.

Another thought has brought relief. We can read it between the lines. It is this: "Do I love my people more than God loves them? Am I willing to do for them more than God will do for them? No! No! God has done for them all that could be done in the past, will do for them all that can be done in the future. The word of God has been effectual. Many, many will be saved. All may be if they will." In this strain he continues until able to express his deliberate thought. "My heart's desire and prayer for Israel is that they might be saved." That is mathematics. It is the translation of the text into the language of lower feeling.

Have you had no experience which throws light on Paul's expression? Have you never felt, "Without my husband, my child, there can be no heaven for me"? Have you never prayed, "Save him, O God! Save him, though I be cast away"? At such a moment you may have uttered illogical, incoherent words. But God understands them. Love's wildest cries are dear to Him. In the letter they contradict, in the spirit they fulfil, the commandment of Him who bade us pray saying, " Thy will be done," — who taught us it is his will that not one should be lost of those whom He has given us by the title-deeds of love.

An inferior, self-conscious spirit could not have spoken as Paul spoke. Paul himself could speak thus only when the unutterable vision had fused his soul and burned away its dross. The nearest approach to this glowing utterance was made by Moses when he too had been closeted with God, had talked with God as a man talketh with his friend, had caught enough of the divine spirit to think of others more than of himself. Then for an instant he forgot who had taught him to love and to sacrifice; for that instant fancied he loved men more than God loved them, and exclaimed in substance, " If thou wilt not forgive them, blot me, I pray thee, out of the book which thou hast written." Moses had left the divine presence but a little moment when he lost power to speak such words.

Spoken deliberately, they would be blasphemy. Spoken in the supreme moment when the heaven-kindled heart melts the fetters of the intellect, they are doxologies. If we picture God in the image of a small-souled, jealous lover, of course we shall count such language blasphemous. If we remember that God is God, it will seem prayer.

That little boy was set by you, his parent, to protect his infant sister. He did so well the duty you assigned him that, when you had occasion to punish his charge, he forgot that you were wiser and tenderer than he. For an instant, while his brain's small eye was dazzled by the light from his heart, he thought he must protect her even from you! He asked: "Mother, let Mary go with us, or let me stay with her. I cannot go without her." Did that anger you? Did it provoke you to say " If my boy loves his sister better than his mother, she will leave him "? If so, it was not because you are like God. When John Knox cried in an agony, " Give me Scotland or I die!" was he not setting his will against the Eternal? Was it not his business to live and work willingly, though it should not be God's purpose to give him Scotland? The dictionary and grammar books answer " Yes!" What God himself thought of John Knox's prayer you may read in the way He answered it.

Paul simply felt about eternal things as all honorable men feel about temporal things. Offer your body's life for another's, plunge into the sea to rescue a drowning man, and right-minded men will call you " hero." To offer your soul's life, if that were possible, to save your brother from eternal death, — were that less heroic? There are times when men should count the cost of their resolves. The Master said it. But there are times when only cowards can be prudent; times when, if one counts the cost, he is a caitiff.

Troy is burning, her army is scattered, her monarch slain. Foes fill her streets. The gods bid Æneas fly. On him rests the last hope of his people. The priests with the sacred image, the company of men, women, and children in his charge, hear the furious cries of the approaching Greeks. They urge Æneas to instant flight. But within the walls of Troy Æneas' father waits. He is an old man and useless. Too feeble to walk, but a few days more of life are possible to him. Shall Æneas delay? Shall he return and risk his life in the attempt to bear the old Anchises on his shoulders, a mark for Grecian swords and spears? Yes! And the gods will veil him in protecting cloud and lead him safely. A hero cannot count the cost when his father is in danger. Even pagans knew that. But Christians are not less self-sacrificing than pagans, but more. Paul could not count the cost when his brethren were in danger. His was the spirit which would plunge into the eternal sea to save an infant sinking there, as promptly as lesser heroes would plunge into the Atlantic.

"I will hold this gate against the Saracens until our ranks can form!" "It will be death, for you are unarmed." "I can die!" "But you are unabsolved. Die thus and you will be damned forever." "I know it, but King Louis will be saved; go bid him arm while I hold the gate." Less than that is less than Christian.

By his own will Christ was delivered for our offences. If he had weighed his sacrifice in any other scales than those which mothers use, he never would have made it. What are you and I and all men worth, compared to the infinite God, blessed for evermore? We have no language to express such things. But we know there are millions and millions of worlds, so many that our earth is a grain of sand among them.

If it were annihilated, none but God would know. Christ made all worlds. From Him all gather life and light. Our little sand-grain was peopled by mites that fought against their Creator, set their puny wills defiantly against the Highest, and planted for themselves eternal misery. As our dark and pygmy-peopled earth darts through the shining spaces, its angel with veiled face crying, "These are they who crucified the Lord of Glory," can the universe believe that the Most High will give himself for such an atom? Yet God will sacrifice himself for us because He is God. Were you the only man that ever sinned, Jesus Christ would die for you, because He weighs himself in the same scales He has given mothers and taught mothers to employ.

Friends, if we will thus look, not at the Apostle's words, but through them into the Apostle's soul, we shall see what made him different from us; what made him an apostle; what made him like his Saviour. We shall see a man who thought first of his Master; second of his Master's work; third, or not at all, of his own felicity.

Paul's dialect is strange to us because we have lost his spirit. The language of self-seeking, which in earthly matters we call cowardly, passes current with us for celestial speech. We have thought of religion as a fleet of life-boats. Leap into them, cut away from the sinking vessel, row hard each for himself, — this has been long the cry. It was not the cry of Paul. It was not the cry of Moses. Their work was to tow the ship to harbor.

To go to heaven alone! That would not be possible for such men. To them the thought was terrible. Their love of God quintupled their love of men. Therefore these men were trees full of sap. The faster they grew heavenward, the deeper and broader grew the roots with which they grasped the earth.

I think a man's religion, like most else within him, often begins in selfishness. If it is true religion, it cannot end in selfishness.

The child sees in his mother at first only the reservoir of food and comfort. He seeks her bosom for his own sake. By and by he will love her in another way. Not what he can gain from her, but what he can do for her, then becomes his quest.

"What must I do to be saved?" That is often the sinner's first cry. With only that he may come to Christ. If he tarries with Jesus the cry will change into "What may I do to save?" That is the cry which opens the gates of heaven. It is the only cry which can give victory over the world, or keep the disciple near the Master. He who fights the battle filled with the spirit that flashes through the text will end his warfare with the shout of trumpet-toned triumph: "I have fought the good fight, I have finished the work thou gavest me to do."

XVI.

EASTER: TRANSFIGURATION.

And after six days Jesus taketh with him Peter, and James, and John, and bringeth them up into a high mountain apart by themselves; and he was transfigured before them. — MARK ix. 2. (R. V.)

THE last clause of the text should, I think, be read, not "He was *transfigured* before them," but "He was transfigured before *them*." For the fact which Mark would make prominent is not that Jesus was transfigured, but that he was transfigured in the presence of certain witnesses.

1. The reading I suggest is favored by the Greek laws of emphasis.

2. The fact it brings to light is corroborated by many intimations in the Gospels.

3. The lessons it reveals the Master teaching are precisely those which Peter, James, and John appear to have supremely needed at that critical time when this transfiguration occurred.

I. Transfiguration does not seem to have been an unusual experience with our Lord.

We read of several occasions when He assumed an appearance which inspired unusual awe in those who beheld Him. There were times when even the disciples, accustomed though they were to familiar intercourse with Jesus, "durst not ask Him any questions." When, with a whisp of straw, He drove the money-changers from the temple, the subjection of the crowd to a single man, and He the man of whom they had lightly spoken as only "the carpenter's son," is best explained by supposing that they saw in Him a supernal majesty. When the multitude led by soldiers approached Gethsemane to apprehend Him, — remember He had come directly from communing with heavenly beings, — there was something in the appearance of the solitary and defenceless One which moved them to draw back and fall upon the ground in attitude of worship.[1] I do not infer that on these occasions

[1] It is possible that the same soldiers who arrested Jesus at Gethsemane were on guard during his trial before Pilate. If so, the touch of rancor in their mocking may have been caused by their vivid recollection of the homage they had been unconsciously constrained to pay Him the preceding night. The scarlet robe and the crown of thorns may be proofs of the profound awe felt by the Roman soldiers before Him who the next day appeared

our Lord appeared altogether as He was seen upon the mount, but that his appearance was the same in kind, though less in degree; that a change occurred which affected beholders with the awe expressed by Peter when he spoke, "not knowing what he said;" an awe which made men fear to gaze or to intrude upon Him.

Again, that Jesus went apart by himself into mountains to pray, we are told in a way that implies this to have been his custom. No mortal eyes observed Him at those times of solitary communion with his Father. But on more than one occasion we are told that angels came and "ministered" to Him; "strengthened Him," "comforted Him." Keep these facts in mind. Remember that they were known to the narrator; remember also that on every other occasion when Jesus went "apart to pray," He dismissed his disciples and went alone, and read with the right emphasis, " And after six days Jesus taketh with Him Peter, and James, and John, and leadeth them up into a high

---

to them an ordinary man. In coarse natures the reaction from extreme reverence to none at all is generally vindictive. Those Frenchmen who had bowed lowest before the crown compelled their king to wear the red cap.

mountain apart by themselves and was transfigured *before them.*"

To my mind the implication of the narrative is plainly this: "Jesus was accustomed to go apart to pray, — to ascend mountains and spend whole nights in devotion. He was accustomed to meet heavenly beings there. He was accustomed to shine among them as the light. All this we know. But once He took three earthly witnesses, and permitted them to see those angels, who "strengthened Him," "comforted Him," "ministered unto Him." Some at least of these celestial visitors were seen to be pious men who had lived and tried to do God's will on earth. One of them certainly had died and been buried as we must be.

The Transfiguration appears to have been an event in the line of our own experience.

We know something of the power exerted by the soul in changing the appearance of the body. If you heard that your child was dead, your face would blanch. If you were told your dying child would recover, your face would shine. The man who cherishes impure thoughts will in due time reveal them in his countenance. Love and purity illuminate the darkest features; malice and foul imaginations darken the most luminous ones. But the face is not only the door-plate on which are written the names of those that occupy the house: it is the window through which they peer. When one is suddenly relieved from mental anguish, or roused by rapturous thoughts, we can find no more accurate word to describe the change that occurs in his appearance than to say, " He seemed transfigured."

Do not these familiar facts help us towards conceiving what transforming energy a soul like Christ's must have exerted upon a body such as his, while He was conversing with celestial beings?

There are well-attested instances where, just before death, the veil of sense between the two worlds has seemed to be withdrawn, and the dying has called the name of some loved one long departed. Then the pale, worn features shone with a light never seen in them before; friends ceased to weep and felt, " It is good for us to be here." I do not mean to assert that the dying one actually beheld the face of the returning dead. I do not know. But what no one can deny is the power with which the soul — awakened by some unusual experience — transfigured the sick face.

Now think of this lantern. Its sides are daubed with paint and grime. Through them the tallow dip within can send only a few feeble rays. When it blazes with unaccustomed brilliancy, a few more rays are transmitted. Such lanterns are we. Our bodies are coarsened and dulled by our disobedience to the laws of their development and preservation. The soul within smoulders, barely burning. Yet such souls as ours can shine through bodies like ours with the effulgence which you may have seen when your dying mother thought she saw the spirit of your father, for whom she had longed and waited twenty years.

Look upon this lantern. Its sides are unflecked crystal. No stain dims their transparency. Each ray of the Drummond light that blazes within them is perfectly transmitted. Such a light in such a body was Jesus Christ, when his soul had been kindled by converse with Moses and Elias upon the theme which at his birth made heaven sing.

II. What lessons did Christ mean to teach his disciples by going thus once into his closet without having shut to the door?

1. He showed them the source of his strength. How often do we read that in his devotions angels " strengthened Him "? In solitude, when temptation had come and He had retired into the wilderness to seek divine help against it; in Gethsemane, before enduring the trial and the crucifixion ; at other times, when He had sought seclusion with his Father to prepare himself for what must come, " an angel strengthened Him."

Such seasons of communion with Heaven are needed by his disciples. If we live in this world alone, we shall be smothered by its small horizon. We need experiences which remind us that we are citizens of eternity, — experiences which will make the events of the markets, of the grave-yard, and even wars and rumors of wars, seem insignificant except so far as they move us to consider the " sign of the Son of Man."

When Elisha asked for a double portion of Elijah's spirit, Elijah answered, "If thou shalt see me when I am taken from thee it shall be so, as thou desirest. But if not it shall not be so." If we think only of the body, we are on the road to saying, " Let us eat and drink, for to-morrow we die." While we discern those who have gone before, we are moved to reason, "Let us watch and pray, for to-morrow we live."

2. Christ strengthened his disciples to meet the trouble that was coming, by showing them what that trouble meant.

Observe the context. In each of the evangelists it is the same. Peter confesses Christ. Then Jesus foretells his own crucifixion. Peter protests against the shame of it. Christ replies, " He that is ashamed of me and of my words, of him shall the Son of Man be ashamed when He cometh with all the holy angels." Then to the twelve he continues: "Some of you standing here shall not see death until you behold the Son of Man in his glory." Each of the three evangelists who record it dates the Transfiguration from this conversation, as if the scene on the mount were in some way connected with it. And was it not? On the mount, three of those "standing here" did see Christ in his glory. In the first chapter of his Second Epistle, Peter explicitly describes this as the occasion upon which he had seen the Son of Man "in his glory." And as the three listened to the speech of heaven, what was the theme? The same which they had discussed "eight" or "six" days before. The thing of which the three blind mortals had been ashamed, and one of them had said, "Far be it from thee!" is the thing in which Heaven glories! The thing of which Heaven would be ashamed is the thing in which these disciples would glory.

Is it not plain that the three who most needed this lesson were Peter, who had protested most vehemently against the cross, and James and John, the throne-seekers?— Peter, who will take the sword to assault the high priest's servant, and the Sons of Zebedee, who would call down fire from heaven after the manner of Elijah before he learned to understand the power of Christ revealed in the still small voice.

Did not these most need to be taught that the throne of God was the cross?

3. But why did the Master forbid the three to mention the heavenly interview until after He should arise from the dead? Plainly a prominent purpose of the peculiar experience granted them was, to impress their minds with a consciousness of the sympathy of the two worlds. The scene must have made them feel that heaven and earth were adjacent mansions in their Father's

house; that the door was always swinging. As their Master retired at will into celestial companionships, so might they. But this was a lesson they did not need to use while He, their Guide, their Friend, their Saviour, was with them in the world. " Hear ye Him ! " was the sole direction they required then.

But the time was drawing near when they would need to use the lesson learned upon the mount. That time was not when Jesus hung upon the cross, not even when his body lay in the sepulchre, but when He had risen, and they would be tempted to believe that their continued communion with Him was an illusion, an " idle tale." But most of all would they need to realize the nearness of heaven and earth after the Lord had ascended up out of their sight; when they had seen Him vanish in the cloud, and felt the fancy assailing them, and wrapping itself around them like a fog, that He had gone far off beyond the stars, and left them to fight their way alone up to his distant throne.

When that time came, and come to them it did, as it comes to us, the seal of silence was broken. Then they might " comfort one another with these words," and tell all men that Christ holds heaven and earth together; that the dead join hands with the living around Him, for He who is always with them, is always with us even unto the end of the world.

It is when we are in the furnace heated seven times hotter than it is wont to be heated that we most need to see beside us, and unharmed by the fire, the form of the Fourth. It is when Death has taken away our loved ones and we know not where he has laid them, that we most need to see Moses and Elias standing with Jesus upon the shining mount.

XVII.

FLOWER SUNDAY.

To Children.

Consider the lilies of the field, how they grow. — MATT. vi. 28.

THERE are three virtues which Jesus was endeavoring to teach when He told his disciples to consider the lilies. They are, contentment, obedience, humility.

I. Flowers are not only beautiful, but they always seem contented and glad. Did you ever think how little they have to make them so? They live on other people's leavings. The air gives them only what finer folks reject and call poison. When the birds and the beasts have taken from the atmosphere all they want, the flowers, like poor Lazarus, desire what is left, the crumbs that fall from the rich man's table. Then, too, if there is any dreadful filth from the sewers or the barnyard, of which men do not know how else to be rid, they give it to the flowers;

just as I have seen certain children send ragged clothes and broken toys to the Christmas poor-box. But the flowers are grateful, and though they cannot talk they blush with gratitude, pink or blue or yellow or white, according to the color of their blood. Then the poor flower-folk, out of these odds and ends which nobody else will have, make for themselves such splendid clothes as King Solomon could not get, though he had first choice of everything, and all the weavers and tailors and jewellers in the world to dress him.

Once there was a toy chariot in a shop window. It had two horses, a driver, and four people inside. It went by springs, and when it moved the horses pranced, the driver cracked his whip, and the people inside craned their necks to see what was the matter. There was a certain boy who thought he would be perfectly happy if he only had that chariot. He longed for it, and talked about nothing else for weeks. At last Christmas came, and some one gave him a brown-paper parcel, tied with a long piece of pack-thread. It was the long-coveted chariot. The boy danced with delight as he tore open the paper and tossed away the thread. Wise auntie picked up the thread from the floor and said, "May I have this?"

Not many evenings afterwards the boy was asking for something to play with. "Why don't you get your chariot?" "Oh, I am sick and tired of that!" Then wise auntie took out of her bag the piece of pack-thread which he had flung away. She taught the owner of the chariot to play cat's-cradle with the twine. She taught him the names of the figures as they appeared, triangles and parallelograms and squares. She taught him how to bring out new figures. Many a long winter's evening seemed short to them both as they played with that string. The boy never seemed to tire of it, and from it he learned with delight many a lesson that helped him at school and on the play-ground, too. But the most important of them was, that an old string well used could give a hundred-fold more pleasure than even a gilded chariot which could only be looked at and coveted.

My boy had a beautiful Chinese top which spun itself. He wearied of it in a few days. But for three seasons he has been happy with an old peg-top that cost five cents, but which nobody can spin without a deal of practice. I never knew a girl kept happy long by a silk dress made at the mantua-maker's, but to make a gown of calico with her own hands will give any girl real and permanent delight.

Some of you may be studying geometry. It often seems tedious and stupid. That everlasting $A\,B\,C$; $X\,Y\,Z$; and two parallel lines between two other parallel lines are equal, etc. "What if they are? Who cares? I'd rather fly my kite." That is because you keep on trying to gain more knowledge without getting the good out of the knowledge you have. Go into the yard. Take a shingle, a short string, a lead pencil, and a yardstick. Find out with these the distance between the back door-sill and the top of the next house. When you have succeeded you will enjoy geometry; you will understand that we could have no railroads, nor bridges, nor Atlantic cables, and could never learn how far it is to anywhere much beyond the ends of our noses, if it were not for those stupid triangles and parallelograms.

Sometimes the Sunday-School lessons and even the sermon grow tedious, especially in summer. You get tired of hearing "Blessed are the merciful." That, too, is because you don't use what you know. Carry that knowledge about mercy somewhere and use it. Try to be merciful in collecting beetles and butterflies. Try to catch trout without hurting them, — you cannot do it with worms, but you can with a fly, — and you will begin to enjoy the sermon.

So the first lesson in contentment is to get all the good out of the things you have, before you wish for more things.

II. Flowers have no wings and no feet. They must stay in one place. Therefore they never do anything which they cannot do at home.

I will tell you a parable. A boy lived in the country. He was happy as the day was long. He played in the fields. He ran home at dinner and at supper time, and told his mother everything he saw and everything he did. But one day he overheard the beasts talking together. The horses stood under a shady tree watching him, and he thought they said: "Poor boy! he has only two feet: how tired he must get!" But one old circus horse, who had been turned out to die, said: "Oh, no! He has four feet, but his mother whips him if he does n't walk on his hind-legs! I know how to pity him."

While he listened to the beasts, somehow the boy began to grow ashamed. So he got down on his hands and knees and tried to walk that way. He was very tired when he reached home. But though his mother asked him how his trousers got so muddy and torn, he only hung his head and would not tell.

One evening he was late, from going on all-fours. The bats were flitting around, and he heard them say: "Poor boy! he has to spend the best part of his time in bed. At night, when it is so splendid to be out, he has to be shut up." The next day he heard the crows, that steal corn and eat carrion, cawing: "Poor boy! he has to eat cooked corn and tough meat. How his jaws must ache!" Thus he began to pity himself and fancy he was very wretched, and that his mother meant to make him miserable. So he stayed out nights and began to eat carrion. He grew peaked from never walking upright, and from getting scared so often in the darkness, and from the dreadful carrion which he smoked and chewed and drank. But when his mother asked what ailed him he would not tell. He went to the owl about it, who looked so wise. She said his trouble all came of too much sunlight, and he must put out his eyes or he would never be any better. So he put out his eyes. He came no more to church or Sunday School. He could not see to find his mother, even if he had wanted to. He was seen last Sunday in a dram-shop. I don't know where he is now, but he is very forlorn.

The flowers told him long ago: "Never do anything you cannot do at home; never do anything you are ashamed to do at home." If a boy will stick to that, he will grow up like a flower into a noble and beautiful man. When the Lord Jesus was asked to do wrong he said: "I and my Father are one." It was his way of saying, "That is not as they do at home; therefore I cannot do so here."

If boys use their feet to get away from home, they are worse off than the flowers, which have no feet. But if they use them to carry their homes wherever they go, they are far more blessed than the fairest flowers.

III. The flowers have no tongues. I do not mean that you must not talk. God has given us tongues, and means us to use them. But let the silent beauty of the flowers teach us to do all the good we can and make no fuss about it. Never be in a hurry to tell people you are Christians, but act so that they cannot help finding it out.

Did you ever watch beans grow? They come out of the ground as if they had been planted upside down. Each appears carrying the seed on top of his stalk, as if they were afraid folks would not know they were beans unless they immediately told them. But most flowers wait patiently and humbly to be known by their fruits.

Sometimes boys get laughed at because they think they must tell everybody that they are Christians. They talk about their piety, and never show it in any other way. But no boy gets laughed at for *being* a Christian; for being true and brave and kind and humble and pure, like the Lord Jesus.

Consider the lilies, and see if you can read, with the help of this sermon, the words written upon their leaves: Contentment, Obedience, Humility.

XVIII.

DECORATION DAY.

For here have we no continuing city, but we seek one to come. — HEB. xiii. 14.

MAN is distinguished from all other denizens of earth by his inclination to build sepulchres. I recall no other human industry which is not rooted in some instinct shown by the inferior creatures. Beavers build cities. Bees maintain a civil polity. Ants plant and reap; organize municipalities with hospitals for the sick; support schools in which the young are taught to earn their living. Wolves combine in regiments, and, officered by corporals and generals, prosecute campaigns which manifest both strategy and discipline. There are insects which weave garments and wear them, build houses and dwell in them, set traps and feed themselves from them. But among the lower creatures I can find no germ of that instinct which seeks to make provision for the dead; no trace of the impulse which moves to act as if the dead could be influenced by its action; no feeblest sign that indicates expectation of a city yet to come.

But from man the indications of that instinct are never absent. All his tribes have left memorials which show him caring for the dead even more sedulously than for the living. His sepulchres outlast his palaces. The homes in which the Incas dwelt have left no vestiges; their tombs endure. Most of the treasures of antiquity which enrich museums are gifts once placed by affection in hands that were cold, or laid upon breasts that were still. The richest, the grandest, and the loveliest structures reared by human hands have been given to the dead. The Mausoleum and the Taj Mahal, the Pyramids and The Gazneh, St. Peter's and the minster of Cologne, the monument to Washington and the tomb beside the Seine, alike bear witness to the existence, in all ages and among all races, of the instinct which has led us to spend one day of every year in strewing flowers upon the graves of those we love.

Animals have never, men have always, acted as if they believed their dead were still alive and sensitive to the ministries of affection. The Egyptians placed guide-books in their sepulchres; Greece put money in the hands of the dead; the earlier Semites gave them both food and money; while the Hebrews covered them with spices.

This instinct of immortality, — call it dream or fancy or faith or superstition, — which has never been detected in the beast, and has never been missing in man, appears to me profoundly significant. Each of us carries in his heart the key to its interpretation. He who brought life and immortality to light reveals the door into the lock of which that key fits with unerring accuracy.

Perhaps this universal and distinctive human instinct has never found a fairer form of expression than in our Decoration Day, which, though cradled in war, has become a strong guardian of peace. Let us therefore listen to some of the suggestions it enforces.

I. By covering graves with flowers we are led to think of death as God intends that we should.

The young rarely think of it at all. Some reach manhood without having learned the meaning of the word. The child hears of many that "they are dead." He may even have seen some die before he tastes the bitterness of death. But each one's hour must come. In due time that friend is taken whose going puts out the light of the one who is left. The earth will never again seem to him as it has seemed. For a little while others remember and respect his grief. Soon they begin again to act and to talk altogether as they used to do. He finds himself wondering, not that to him all is so changed, but that to others life seems still the same. Men go on buying and selling, smiling and weeping, when the things they mind so much seem to him so infinitely trivial. Of dying he has thought as of a thing utterly dreadful. He has joined in the general opinion, and recognized in death the ultimate horror. When he wished to express extremity of repugnance he, too, has been wont to say: "I had rather die than do it!" But the experience which made him for the first time appreciate death as an inexorable fact, and which made him realize that he himself must die, has also robbed death of all terror.

Such is the goodness of God that usually men are first made to feel that they must die, in a way that removes their fear of dying. Yesterday, when the happy child was at play, if you could have convinced him that he had but a few hours to live, you would have plunged him into despair. But, thank God, yesterday you could not make him realize the brevity of life. A lifetime seemed an eternity to him. But to-day God has told him the truth, but has told it as Jesus told his disciples: "I go to prepare a place for you." For to-day the child returns from his mother's grave and buries his head in her bare pillow. The whisper, "In a little while death will take you to her," is not a gloomy threat, but a radiant promise.

So does God, in the rule, prepare men to die by teaching them — if they will learn the lesson — that they are citizens of another country. Every precious grave becomes a certificate of naturalization in the land where our loved ones are. Gradually, to most good men, the time arrives when they feel as the man in Ireland feels when one by one his kindred have gone to America and he is left alone among strangers. The fatherland is still dear, but home is across the sea. So God means us to ripen for heaven as life wears away.

II. We shall best prepare for the life which now is and for that which is to come, if we pause at times to commune with the dead.

They who tell us we should think only of the living and the present, contradict God's gospel, and bid us trample under foot that peculiar sentiment which distinguishes men from brutes. If we obey them, we shall come to resemble brutes in more respects than one.

Let our memories of the departed make us kinder to those who are with us.

The bitterest drop in the cup of bereavement is the recollection of what we might have done but did not do; of what we might have left undone but did. The unkind word, so little recked of once, comes back to sting us when we cannot make atonement.

The deeds of kindness we have done fall back, like drops of rain from the heaven of memory, upon the heart that thirsts in the desert of its loneliness. For more than twenty years before my father's death I was away from home. During all those years I think I did not ten times fail to send a Sunday letter to him. When he had gone each of them was found in the private desk where he had kept his treasures. It was a little thing to do. But —

"The world is wide, these things are small;
They may be little, but they are all."

Mothers, fathers, sons, daughters, sisters, brothers, husbands, wives, you do not yet know how dearly you love each other! Only death can teach you that. You cannot conceive how your hearts will bleed when one is taken and you are left; yet how many days are allowed to pass without one deed of kindness done, one word of tenderness spoken! Your circle will be broken. Not together, but one by one, you must go, and those who remain must live again the past; must live it again in all but this, that you can never say, "I am sorry!"

"She was the flower of my house. She gave my life its beauty and its fragrance. But I returned her neither sunshine nor dew. My frowns I brought home to those who were saddened by them, my smiles I wasted among those who cared not for them. And now she has gone! — she has gone!" That is the future many are preparing for themselves.

III. This day should inspire in us gratitude towards our fathers, and incite us to emulate their example.

To more than half of those now living our civil war is only history. Young men know it as they know the Revolution. Many whose parents fell in its battles cannot recall the faces of those parents. They are strangers to the sentiment which swayed the nation twenty-five years ago. Therefore to them those who remember should speak.

This country of ours seemed given over to pleasure-seeking and money-making. More than three millions of its citizens were held in slavery. Good men deplored the fact, but none could find the remedy. A vast majority continued buying and selling, marrying and giving in marriage, as if the infamy did not in the least concern them. Almost no one appeared to care for his country except as a mine out of which to dig treasure for himself. Americans talked calmly of the rupture of the Union. They discussed the expediency of such a course, and the gains or losses that probably would come of carving into morsels our fatherland. Of patriotism there seemed none.

At last cannon were fired at fort Sumter. Mr. Lincoln called for seventy-five thousand men to volunteer as soldiers. The number seemed to us, who heard the call, enormous. He asked with fear and trembling.

Then the Spirit of the Lord moved upon our people. From Maine to California, men forgot to care for their money or their lives. In every state and city and village the same resolve was registered: "Our country shall be saved." Old and young, women and children, quivered with the high enthusiasm. Was any individual suspected of caring for his own interest, for his property or his life, more than for the salvation of his country, women would not speak to him! He was shamed, if not into his duty, at least into pretence of his duty.

For four years, young men, we breathed the atmosphere of heroic self-sacrifice. During four years the common feeling among Americans was this: "My country owns me! Whatever she requires of me, that I am to do. It is not for me to ask, 'Where can I earn wealth? Where can I win power? Where can I enjoy life? but Where can I be useful to her?'"

Certainly there were hypocrites among us. But their hypocrisy bore witness to the prevalence of virtue. For such were the sentiments dominant among your fathers that those who did not care for their country felt constrained to feign what they did not feel. Women sent their sons and their husbands to die, and did not murmur.

Such was the spirit of your fathers during four solemn, splendid years. Because that spirit animated them you have still a country. That passion of self-sacrifice God gave unto your elders, which taught them they were here to live, not for themselves, but to live and if need be to die for others, has secured for you this superb inheritance.

And you, young men, are called by the same God to act the same part in peaceful times. I frankly tell you, yours is the harder task. For you are set to stand in business, in politics, in society, in church, in family, realizing that you are not your own, that you are here to do, not what is profitable or what is pleasant to yourselves, but what is right, what God and your neighbors need to have you do. Only so can you maintain what your fathers won. You are helped by no tide of popular enthusiasm which will carry you forward in its rush. The current sets against you. It is always harder to live for the right than to die for it. But unless in time of peace we obey the Spirit who moved our fathers in time of war, we shall help our nation to become a rabble of quarrelling shop-keepers, of factory operatives who twine hemp for their own execution.

Let us ask ourselves, while we breathe the perfumes that fill the air, " What am I doing for any other than myself? Am I living only for my own pleasure, for my own profit? Can I look without shame upon these granite statues! Dare I lay garlands upon the graves of those who fell at Gettysburg and in the Wilderness ? "

IV. To the elders among us, this day brings brightest witness to the guardian care of God.

You remember days when the most hopeful dared not hope to witness the end of slavery in our land. We remember how God forced us, by means which seemed so cruel and have proved so kind, to do right. We tried for years and years to save ourselves without saving our country, and could not. Then we tried to save our country without saving freedom, and we could not. When at last we were compelled to do right, we trembled and believed that generations must pass before the savage passions fed by war could be extinguished. We were sure a standing army would be requisite to hold the South to allegiance ; that the land would be bankrupted by its debt; would be drowned in ignorance by the black man's vote. But none of these things came to pass. The soldiers of the South met the soldiers of the North as brothers. The debt began to melt away, and the nations to recognize that the baptism of fire and of blood had given us a right to stand among the foremost.

And still we have little faith! We are not worthy to carry flowers to these graves; we are not worthy to tell our children of the great deeds we remember, nor to bear the name of the Christ who has died for us, — unless we can gather, from the revelation He unveils in Decoration Day, hope and courage that will enable us to look boldly into the eyes of political chicane, of intemperance, of municipal rings, of Antichristian combinations and infidelities of every sort, and say to them all, " We will destroy you! By the help of God, we are stronger than you! "

Rejoice, ye righteous! Lift up thy voice, O America! lift it up with strength. Be not afraid. Cry unto the cities of our country, " Behold your God! "

XIX.

HARVEST SUNDAY.[1]

And Isaac went out to meditate in the field at eventide. — GEN. xxiv. 63.

I. THESE fruits remind us that our Father has provided for us food abundantly.

1. They bear witness that He has not only given us provision for a day, as charity visitors give meals to paupers, but that He provides for us a steady income. Year after year He causes the earth to give bread to the eater and seed to the sower. In Isaac's day it was not so. Then, a local drought or an untimely frost produced a famine and the people starved. In our day the prayer of Christ has been so far fulfilled that in material things at least, the whole of Christendom is one. Unless the harvests fail the

---

[1] In accordance with the yearly custom at Berkeley Street Church, the pulpit platform was covered with vegetables, fruits, and flowers, which had been contributed by individuals for the general use. These, together with offerings of meat and money, were to be distributed before Thanksgiving Day as the officers of the church should direct.

same year over all the earth — which they never do — there can be no famine among Christian nations. Steam has lengthened their arms. If Russia is hungry, she is fed from the lap of America.

2. Consider further that God so gives as to ennoble the recipients of his charities by cultivating in them manly independence. The most difficult task we have to perform is to relieve the poor without degrading them. But God supplies our needs in ways that elevate us.

Food is not brought to us in baskets and set down before our doors. God might feed us by sending aerial ships, ferried by angels across the sky, with freights of food for all. By that means He would pauperize and make the world a colossal Ireland. Therefore He does not feed us so. No good apple ripens but some man feels that he himself has made it, and finds in the food, whether he has raised it or bought it, the result of his own exertion. God is so careful not to pauperize men by his charities that, though every morsel is God's gift as really as it would appear to be if his hand were visible bestowing it, men feel and are meant to feel that they themselves produce what they consume. So much more careful is our Maker of our characters than of his own reputation, that He never forces his agency on our attention. We must reflect before we can realize that we owe Him gratitude. There is need of occasions like this to remind the farmer who grows wheat that he does not grow it by himself. As a wise mother guides the unskilled fingers of her child to move aright over the paper she holds in place the pencil she has given him, and rejoices to hear him say, " Charlie can make pictures! " so, carefully, God cultivates in us the germs of self-reliance.

3. Each object here, while it represents ennobling human labor, reminds us also of the wealth of gladness God has already made these fruits the means of bestowing upon men. We are accustomed to dwell upon the pleasure of consuming the products of the earth. We consider too little the pleasure of producing them. When you see a genial company enjoying their Thanksgiving dinner, remember that the preparation of it has given others a larger sum of satisfaction than the present company receives. Consider the joy of wholesome exercise experienced by the sower going forth to sow; the thrill in some one's soul when he saw the

blades appear, and read in the tasselled grain the prophecies of coming harvests; the sweet sleep of the laboring man; the beauty of sky and earth perpetually pressing upon the reapers, and filling with quiet rapture those who, having eyes, will see! Innumerable insects have danced in ecstasy of innocent intoxication over the blossoms whose beauty feeds the faith of every man who will, as we are told to do, consider the lilies. But the chief felicity of man comes from succeeding in good work. Every ripened apple, every grain of wheat, registers the success of some one in a good work; is the writing of the Master, " Well done, good and faithful servant."

4. Consider the spiritual treasures of strengthened character each harvest represents! The moral condition of a people is accurately gauged by the quality of their agriculture. A consummate Lawton blackberry is a more certain evidence than a prayer-meeting that the basilar Christian virtues have been at work in a community. An excellent Antwerp raspberry was never grown until self-denial, resolute faith, patience of hope created it; while there have been prayer-meetings which failed to de-

monstrate the presence of either self-denial, patience, or faith. Neither cannibals nor Sybarites ever produced a Bartlett pear, nor ever will. No general statement is truer than this, that a thriftless agriculture evinces a degraded moral state. Turkey, with a soil of exquisite fertility, is always hungry. Poor, sterile Norway and Sweden export grain. "Seek ye first the kingdom of God and his righteousness, and all these things shall be added unto you." God put man into the garden to till it and to dress it. If man obeys, God's earth returns a rich reward. If he disobeys, man always reaps thorns and thistles. This is true in all climates and under all meridians. Therefore the excellence of their fruitage is a just reason for confidence in the moral character of any people. It is a better test than the speeches of their legislators, the books of their authors, or even the wisdom of their laws. In a nation thoroughly corrupted, genius may blaze as it blazed in Demosthenes and in Cicero, but the harvests will fail as they failed in Greece and in Rome. The punishment perpetually threatened upon the Jews was that, if they forsook God, blight and mildew would devour their fields.

Among all peoples the same retribution has ultimately followed persistent disobedience of God.

The first words legible upon these harvest fruits are therefore: "Thank God, who feeds us. Thank Him that in feeding He does not pauperize us. Thank Him that He mingles joy with the procuring as richly as with the consuming of his gifts. Thank Him, above all, for the evidence brought by these full harvests recurring every year that, beneath the surface-wickedness of our national life, there is a deep and prevalent endeavor to "fear God and keep his commandments."

If it is seemly to thank God for the corn and the oil, we ought far more to thank Him for the better gifts of morality and faith. Yet religious people shrink from acknowledging God's goodness in keeping them good. They are afraid of appearing self-righteous. Far as our country is from what it ought to be, and from what by God's help we hope to make it, a higher standard of living prevails in the United States than in any other country on the globe. Our prayers and the prayers of our fathers have been answered. When the seeds of one year have produced a hundred fold, the farmer is encouraged to sow more bountifully the next season. So should it be in spiritual husbandry. There has been almost no effort made in America for the sake of Christ and his kingdom which has not been obviously blessed. We have sown few seeds that have not borne sixty fold.

II. These fruits teach us to feel our need of God in ways that impel us to hope and to pray.

By watching the processes of nature, men have inferred, in a way that seems to me illogical, that there is no God. Thinkers whose sincerity I do not question affirm that they can see no need of a God. The laws of nature are invariable, we are told. They are never broken; they cannot be changed; their working furnishes no evidence of a personal Will, reveals no need of one.

But these flowers and fruits seem to me written over with testimonies to the need and the presence of a controlling Will, — a Will altogether independent and outside of what we call the "laws of nature."

Look at this cranberry. It is a child of humble parentage. I have often seen it growing under the laws of nature with no help from a personal will. So growing, it bears bitter little berries no bigger than duck-shot, and so few of them that an acre may produce perhaps two pecks. So you may find them to-day in New Brunswick wilderness or South African savanna.

But a personal will, named Man, has so employed the laws of nature on Cape Cod as to make these poor little bushes bear many barrels, four hundred dollars' worth to an acre, I am told, of such fruit as this.

Here is a luscious apple. It is a child of the crab. Not such a crab as we see in gardens, but a bitter midge of a thing, all skin and core and pucker. It will grow wild almost anywhere between the Cape of Good Hope and Spitzbergen. For all the laws of nature, it continued a wizened, worthless thing, until a controlling will took it in hand and made it a Rhode Island Pippin, a Montreal Fameuse, an Ohio Belle Flower. When the care of man is withdrawn, it begins to relapse into the crab state again, like an unchurched Christian falling from grace.

Look, if you will, at this golden emblem of good-nature, this symbol of contentment in a well-completed destiny, this harbinger of Thanksgiving, this pumpkin. What is it and whence did it come? Who is its father? Who is its mother? And who are its kindred? Is it not the offspring of a wretched gourd that climbed up trees in the edge of jungles, and hung its little lumpy fruit in a bewildered way among the branches, as if it did not know why it was made, and hoped some one would see it and tell it what to do?

And at last some one did see, — the Egyptians, I am told. They took it and taught it what to do, and, obeying the education given by the human will, it became in due time a cucumber, a watermelon, a luscious citron, and, not least if last, the golden ornament of New England cornfields. Finally, by further interference of an independent personal will, it may become a pumpkin-pie.

Yet men who have carefully observed and told us how the human will, by using the laws of nature intelligently, can convert a wretched gourd into a watermelon, while they have seen no instance in which the laws of nature unaided by the human will have wrought so great a change, conclude that natural laws, uncontrolled and undirected by a personal Will, have transformed the harem of Sardanapalus into the Christian family, the quarrelling murderers of Anglia into the English Parliament, the feasting of cannibals into the New England Thanksgiving. That is, while all our studies demonstrate the immense importance of the presence of a personal Will in changing a Shetland pony into a cart-horse, no personal Will can have had place in transforming an ape into Shakespeare.

The studies which have been most popular for many years emphasize the efficacy of man's interference, not in breaking but in applying the laws of nature. By using them man can transform and has transformed black coal into dazzling light, and dock mud into strawberries.

Suppose the voice of prayer should be lifted by the inanimate creation. The coals cannot see him, but they have a tradition which speaks of man and calls him "helper," *i. e.* "holy." The plants cannot see him, but in their hearts the same old story reigns. Moved by the tradition, both coals and mud and plants begin to pray. The black carbon cries, "O man, if there be any man, make me a shining light!" The mud cries, "O man, if there be any man, convert me into strawberries!" The gourd cries, "O man, if there be any man, make me a watermelon!"

These supplications might well seem silly to the unbelievers of their race, but this is accurately the figure I have read you from the Apostle Paul in the eighth chapter of Romans.

The whole creation, he affirms, groans and travails in pain together. The earnest expectation of all other created things waiteth for the revealing, the instructive teaching, of the sons of God, that is, of man redeemed and enlightened by God. The whole creation waiteth for man, by the sovereignty of his redeemed and purified will, to conduct it into its designed development. Creation, that is, all but man, has been made subject to vanity, *i. e.* confusion, aimlessness, not by its own choice, but by reason of God, who thus subjected it in hope that man would redeem it into order; and creation must remain undeveloped until man, by his God-enlightened will, leads it into liberty of glorious development. The crab remains a crab until man makes it an apple; the gourd remains a gourd until man makes it a melon. Neither knows for what it was meant, nor into what it can be made, until it feels and yields to human influence.

In like manner also the Spirit helpeth our infirmities, for we know not what we should pray for as we ought, but the Spirit maketh intercession within us and for us according to the mind of God. The Spirit knows what we need, knows what He intended us to become, and that He alone can make us.

Every soul is a garden of God. We are his planting. To pray to Him, to trust in Him, to hope in Him, to rejoice in Him, is our only wisdom, our only peace.

Therefore the sight of these fruits moves me to pray, for in praying I am only asking One unimaginably better and abler than myself to do for me as I can do for my inferiors and dependents. I do not ask God to break his laws. When I ask a carpenter to smooth a board I ask him not to break his plane, but to use it. Natural laws are God's tools. When I pray I only ask Him to use them as I cannot.[1] I look upon this rose. I remember the scentless, ragged, single blossom which man's care has developed into the tea

---

[1] In accuracy of speech, God's laws are simply God's ways of working. In a man we should call them habits. They are invariable because always the best.

which cheers, the camelia which adorns, and I ask God to do for me and all his human flowers more and better than men have done for roses as He is greater and better than men.

To think of God under his name of "Husbandman" fills me with large hopes. I know how a genuine love for flowers makes a man delight in his garden. He watches with eagerness for the tender blade to appear, struggling out of darkness. He shields it with carefulest care from the perils that threaten its young life. His affection grows with his care. With sweet and honest satisfaction he observes the forming buds. He strives to make each plant finer than any that have been before; and when one bursts into glory of crimson, or purple, or gold, he calls in his friends and neighbors, saying, "Rejoice with me!"

"Ye are God's husbandry."

Let us remember that God thinks of us as of a vineyard in a very fruitful field. Eye hath not seen, we do not know, what we shall be. But his eyes will not slumber, his care will not fail. We may refuse his control. If we reject his gracious help, we must remain wild grapes. But be sure of this: if we will yield to Him, obey his commandments when we know them, receive his Spirit as it is given, we shall some time appear at his right hand, transformed by the renewing of our minds till the change from what we are to what we shall be will immeasurably exceed the change from the sooty coal into the electric light.

XX.

CHRISTMAS.

The mistletoe, which our New England fathers flung contemptuously away, contained a lesson they would have done more wisely to have heeded.

As the story runs, Balder, the god of peace, was so beautiful that all who saw him loved him. When he lay in his cradle, his mother spoke a charm which restrained all created things from harming him. Eventually it became a pastime of the Scandinavian deities to gather around their favorite and hurl missiles at him to provoke his smiles, which were more lustrous than sunbeams. Oak could not bruise him, granite could not wound him, iron could not pierce him. Obedient to Friga's charm, they fell as thistledown upon his body. But the mother forgot to charm the mistletoe. It grew concealed from sight, and seemed too insignificant for notice. When Loke grew envious, he plucked a spray of mistletoe, sharpened it to an arrow's point, and persuaded Hoder, who was blind, to cast it at Balder. The missile flew with fatal aim and heaven was draped in mourning.

In 1644 the Long Parliament decreed that Christmas, which had long been the merriest day of all the year, should be observed as a fast. But the Pilgrims had already written in the journal of the Mayflower: " Dec. 25, 1620 : This day we went on shore, some to fell timber, some to saw, some to rive, and some to carry, so no man rested on that day." Thus they repeated Lady Friga's error. They consecrated all departments of life except its recreations. Those sturdy heroes fancied play too trivial for their notice. They had no time for sports. They forgot that it is never the consciousness of immortality that makes men feel hurried. Only the consciousness of mortality can do that, for he that believeth shall not make haste. I think that many a Christian parent has loved his children, toiled for them, instructed them, prayed with them, given the best hours of his life to them, and seen them sloughed at last in dissipation, solely because he never played with them. Play is the divinely ordained business of childhood. It is generally in the "child garden" that the human spirit learns to eat or to refuse forbidden fruits. Christmas bears witness that "the ministers of salvation" began their work by thronging the air with radiance and song.

The Church in New England has treated amusements as Congress has treated the Indians, and with somewhat similar results. The Indians once were friendly. Our legislators banished them outside the limits of Christian influence, confined them to the society of buffaloes, bears, wolves, rattlesnakes, and Indian agents; have, in consequence, been forced to spend more than seven hundred million dollars to protect the scalps of fifty million white men from the tomahawks of three hundred thousand red ones, and now complain that Indians cannot be civilized. With equal wisdom the Church thrust amusements far beyond her pale, resigned the management of recreations to her enemies, and grieves, with a surprise which would be ludicrous if it were not sad, to see her children scalped when they enter a bowling alley, touch a billiard-cue, take an oar to pull in a regatta, or touch the hand of a maiden to lead her in the dance.

When the Church refused to use her silver nets, Satan stole and made them snares. She reaped the experience of many mothers who wash and dress their children, set them on chairs where their feet cannot touch the floor, and bid them keep still and be good.

> "But the saucy little boy
> Who had no toy
> Did not know what to do;
> So he rumpled his frock,
> And tore his sock,
> And tried to eat his shoe."

Christmas originated in the instinctive protest of the Christian consciousness against asceticism. It came of a half-conscious endeavor to stamp the divine seal upon gladness.

In the fourth century the relation of the Church to the world had come to resemble that which exists to-day. Christianity had become the dominant religion. But the splendid sports of the pagans drew Christian youths into the ring, the theatre, and the temple. To win them thence, the fathers instituted a Christian festival more alluring than those heathen ones which had proved so seductive. The time selected for its celebration proves the bravery of its originators.

The winter solstice, when the days begin to lengthen, as if the eyes of Time dilated while they watched their returning Lord, has always been the part of the year most honored by all systems of nature-worship. At this season the heathen world celebrated its most brilliant rites and its wildest orgies: the Swedes kindling bonfires on their hill-tops, and crowning columns with evergreen for Lady Friga's sake; the Romans were rushing through their streets in the revels of the Saturnalia; Grecian maidens were waving torches on Helicon to Dionysus; Egyptian youths were bringing branches of palm to the temples of Horus; Persians were singing the birth of Mithras; and even Hindoos were shouting their loudest cries to Vishnu. Each of these festivals had come to be defiled by practices it would be unseemly to describe, when, in the midst of this whirl and confusion, where drunkards raved, night-birds screamed, and serpents coiled, the bold fathers planted the cross, called down the dove, set the cradle of Christ, and declared to those various forms of sun-worship, which numbered among their disciples nine twelfths of the Roman Empire, "The babe is the Light of the World."

Gradually the pagan festivals disappeared, supplanted by Christmas. The victor came forth triumphant, adorned with the spoils taken from those she had conquered and superseded. Those spoils she still wears, for most of our Christmas customs are only pagan practices picked from the mire and made clean. Bishop Liberius would have exulted could he have foreseen what has since come to pass, when, in the year 342, he preached at Rome the first Christmas sermon.

Christmas is not only the children's day: it is a memorial of the childhood of Christendom.

Men love to perpetuate the memories of their childhood. We do not banish Robinson Crusoe from our hearts when we have ceased to believe the fiction fact. The religion of one age has often become the poetry of the next. During the Middle Ages Europe was in its imaginative childhood. Beliefs which to us are fancies were then religious creeds. Many of them still linger, half believed, among the peasants of the old world, and give an atmosphere of peculiar sanctity to Christmas Eve.

In parts of Germany the belief still flutters in many a heart that on the Holy Night all nature bloomed with the pristine loveliness of Eden. On its return the heavens still drop healing dews, and the aspen-tree distils a precious balsam. At midnight the maidens of Thuringen enter the gardens robed in white, shake the fruit-trees, and sing : —

> "Sleep not, sleep not little trees!
> The good lady draws nigh!
> The sun's daughter is coming,
> She will give you leaves,
> She will give you flowers,
> She will give you fruits;
> But eye shall not see
> What she hangeth on thee,
> Till summer returns
> And the July sun burns."

On this Holy Night alone of all the year the quivering aspen-tree has rest. For eighteen centuries her leaves have shivered with the guilty consciousness that she furnished wood for the cross of Christ. On Christmas Eve she rests, remembering that she also furnished wood for the Redeemer's cradle. A leafless bough placed in water on St. Andrew's night will blossom Christmas Eve, and roses of Jericho will adorn it all the year. At twelve o'clock the pains of the lost are relaxed, Judas sleeps upon his bed of fire. For an hour Herod ceases to clank his chains. On this night Pontius Pilate's ghost, which has wandered all the year on the summit of Mt. Pilatus vainly striving to cleanse its hands in the water of "Dead Man's Lake," but only generating storms and tempests by the endeavor, rests until the dawn. The Wandering Jew hears no longer the goading voice "Onward, ever onward!" He sinks upon the ground, his black hair blanches, and he slumbers peacefully as a little child. The daughter of Herodias, doomed to spin an eternal dance in circles round the Arctic pole, finds rest on Christmas Eve. Mountains open their sides. The subterranean gnomes cast forth gems and gold, which are washed with the sand down river channels for the use of men. Water drawn this night will change to wine or preserve its sweetness through the year. At twelve o'clock animals are endued with powers of speech and prophecy. The planets stand still while the beasts of the forests kneel in prayer for men. The sound of church bells will be heard wherever a church has stood, though no vestige of its ruins remain. Bread baked in the open air to-night will cure diseases. Lie in a manger and you will see your future. Peel an apple without breaking the skin, swing the strip three times around your head, drop it behind you, and it will form upon the floor the initial of your sweetheart's name. As the apple was in Paradise the source of sorrow, to-night it becomes the harbinger of joy.

Indeed, the apple was always sacred to Venus, and was used by the augurs in divining. Who of us has never taken an apple, named and counted the seeds to forecast the future? One, I love; two, I love; three, I love, I say; four, I love with all my heart; and, five, I cast away; six, he loves; seven, she loves; eight, both love; nine, he comes; and ten, he tarries; eleven, he courts; and, twelve, — suspense is ended.

Fosbrooke tells us how Roman youths made their declarations. They went by night and hung a garland upon the door, behind which the dear one slept. This asked the important question. Then they returned to their bachelor abodes, filliped apple seeds against the ceiling, and from the way in which they fell upon the floor inferred the chances of a favorable reply.

When our children ask for the wish-bones

at dinner, dry them, pull them with each other, and believe that he who gets the longest limb will have his wish, they are imitating Cornelia and Julius Cæsar, for this same thing the Roman augurs taught children to do at the Saturnalia two thousand years ago.

But shadows also lie on the blessed night. Amber is the congealed tears which mermaids weep into the sea on Christmas Eve, because they have no share in the trophies of the time.

> "For this is the day when the fairy kind
>   Sit weeping alone for their hopeless lot,
> When the wood-maiden sighs to the sighing wind,
>   And the mermaiden weeps in her crystal grot.
> For this is the day when a deed was done,
>   In which they have neither part nor share;
> For the children of clay was salvation won,
>   But not for the forms of earth or air."

Malignant spirits are on the watch, and would riot over the earth but for this. The cock crows all night on Christmas Eve, and the wicked imps, who cannot be wise or they would not be wicked, think it continually about to dawn, and are afraid to appear lest the sun may overtake them.

We twine wreaths of holly with the scarlet berries and call them Christmas wreaths.

The Danes taught us to do that. They said Christ's crown was made of holly. When its briers touched his brow they softened into pointed leaves, and the berries which had been white before were dyed scarlet by his blood.

The Thanksgiving mince pie appears to be inherited from Christmas. Originally it contained no meat but mutton, perhaps from deference to the shepherds of Bethlehem. Into it was put all fruits and spices brought from the East, some say in memory of the Wise Men whose gifts came from the Orient. But the truer theory seems to be that the grateful housewife strove to combine, in a thankful offering, all the products of the year from near and far. In England, to suggest the manger, the crust was made oblong in shape.

From Germany comes the Christmas tree. The legend runs that when Eve plucked that unwholesome apple, the fruit fell from the tree of life, its leaves shrank into needle points, its rich green turned sombre. In short, it became the fir-tree, whose evergreen dress beneath the winter snow still marks it as the tree of life.

On the night of Christ's birth the tree

cast off its mournful dress and bloomed again as of old. This legend is reënacted when we take the fir-tree, decorate it with all things bright and beautiful, and hang upon its boughs gifts radiant with love; leaves and fruits for the healing of the nations. Only by miracle was the true nature of the fir-tree learned.

Maturnus was the son of the widow of Nain. He was sent by St. Peter as a missionary to the Gauls upon the Rhine. The Apostle gave him a staff which had been cut from the tree of life. When the pilgrim reached the Black Forest, he leaned his staff against a fir-tree, and went to sleep. When he awoke it had disappeared. It had grown into the trunk, and become once more a branch of the tree of life. While Maturnus searched for his cane there came a little bird from Paradise, alighted on the branch, and sung a song which told him that the staff had found its parent. So he knew that his journey was ended and straightway began to preach.

Our custom of giving presents is borrowed from the Romans. Their usual gift was a small taper of white wax. Love makes light. But in the time of Tacitus the custom had developed so much ostentation that only the wealthiest could afford to meet the expectations of their friends. Fashionable people sometimes bankrupted themselves by making Saturnalia presents, hoping to receive back again more than they gave. The same danger threatens Christmas among us.

These old traditions would not be worth repeating, but for the fact already mentioned. Most of them were once religious creeds. History was shaped by them, as we are shaping history by our strenuous faith in the opposite of the Gospels.

For an illustration, the legend of the Magi may serve. Its influence can be traced through the Middle Ages, and its power in moulding history shown. This is the tradition. The three Wise Men who came from the East bearing gifts were kings. Twelve days were consumed in their journey. This is one of the reasons given for continuing Christmas festivities twelve days, and concluding them with the Twelfth Night of England, or Sylvester Abend of Germany.

The names of the Wise Men were Melchior, Jaspar, Belthazar. Melchior's gift was a golden apple, which had been cast by Alexander from the tribute of the world, and thirty pieces of silver. What became of the apple I do not know, but the history of the money has been preserved. A Chaldean idol of gold was melted and minted by Terah, and the coins, thirty in number, given to his son Abraham. By Abraham they were paid to Ephron the Hittite for the cave in which Sarah was buried. Thence the coins passed into the hands of the Ishmaelite merchants, who with them bought Joseph from his treacherous brothers. To Joseph they were repaid by these same brethren, when they went to Egypt after corn. With the same coins Joseph bought, from the sovereign of Sheba, spices to embalm his father. After lying a few centuries in the imperial treasury they were brought by the Queen of Sheba as a present to Solomon. The king of Arabia plundered them from the Temple in the time of Rehoboam. They remained in Arabia until Melchior, the king of that country, brought them to Mary. When the Holy Family fled to Egypt, Herod's soldiers pursued them closely. They passed a field where a man was sowing wheat. The grain sprang up instantly by miracle. An hour later the soldiers arrived. " Have any fugitives passed this way?" they asked. "Not since that field was sowed!" was the reply. As the grain was ready to harvest, the soldiers turned another way. When Mary saw the miracle, in surprise she dropped the money Melchior had given her. The peasant picked it up, paid it as a votive offering to the temple at Jerusalem, where it remained until given by the high priest to Judas for the betrayal. How the coins became silver, though they had been cast from an idol of gold, I do not know. Perhaps the idol was only plated. It would be encouraging to discover such an evidence that pagans also tried to be thrifty in matters of religion.

In return for their gifts, Mary gave the Wise Men the swaddling clothes, and the three were eventually baptized by St. Thomas. In the fourth century their remains were miraculously discovered by the Empress Helena and removed to Constantinople.

Here the legend ends and history begins. In the Church of St. Sophia reliques supposed to be those of the Wise Men had long been worshipped, when in the twelfth century they were removed to Milan and presented by the Emperor Frederick, in 1164, to Rhinaldus who carried them to his bishopric of

Cologne. Hence the Magi were called the Three Kings of Cologne. King Louis of France, leaving the skulls at Cologne, transported the bones to Paris. Those who visited Paris to worship at their shrine received rings or fragments of ivory or parchment inscribed with the names of the three worthies, usually with some word of benediction added. These were worn about the person as amulets. They were believed to protect the possessor from disease, and were largely used as gifts between friends. From such a practice arose the custom, so common on the continent, of giving Christmas mottoes, the originals of Christmas cards.

A pleasant reminder of this custom I have witnessed at the annual Christmas ball given at Kroll's Gardens, Berlin, upon Sylvester night. Twenty years ago Kroll's was perhaps the largest dancing hall in Europe. It was always crowded at the Sylvester ball. At the first stroke of twelve the music stopped, dancing ceased; the silence was broken only by the clang of the huge bell striking midnight. The revellers looked up and stood as if spell-bound. The stranger lifted his eyes because the rest had done so. Nothing appeared until the air pulsated with the last stroke of twelve. Then a mist appeared to gather on the lofty ceiling, as when one breathes upon the window pane. The mist condenses. It begins to flutter downward as flakes of snow. Slowly the flakes descend. They seem minutes in falling, before they are seen to be bits of tissue paper. Ladies and gentleman stand below, motionless as statues, each braced for a leap. It is a sight to photograph. Gentlemen with orders glittering on their breasts. Ladies in silk and velvet, with diamonds flashing on arm and bosom. Each in attitude of eager expectation. Before the snow fall reaches the floor, the entire company appears bewitched. They leap upwards, they spring on each other's shoulders, they snatch from each other's hands. Each strives to secure the first handful. Though the papers fall thick and fast, few reach the floor. Well bred though one may be, it is scarcely possible for him to escape the contagion, or keep from scrambling with the rest. The politest people take the measles. The papers are Christmas greetings. He who gathers most is counted victor. The mottoes are preserved through the year, not as amulets, but as tokens of good-will and memorials of Christmas.

But we have not reached the end of this legend of the Wise Men. The three skulls have long been preserved at Cologne, their names written in rubies. They were kept in a mimic temple of gold and gems in the most sacred shrine of the ancient edifice. Over them, and because they were there, arose the grandest monument of Gothic art, the mighty minster of Cologne.

In the year 1212, before the present edifice was built, a peasant boy named Nicholas appeared in Cologne. He was twelve years old. He claimed to be a messenger from Jesus Christ to the children of Germany. He said he had been sent to lead them to the Holy Land.

The elders had failed to capture the sepulchre of Christ by swords and spears. Therefore the little ones must win it by their songs. Jesus would divide the sea for them to pass, and teach them songs which should make the walls of Jerusalem fall down and convert the Saracens to his service.

At the spot consecrated by the reliques of the first pilgrims from the East the children gathered. In his childish treble, with the eloquence of complete conviction, the boy proclaimed the glory of the enterprise. He pointed to the golden casket which enclosed the reliques of the Wise Men. His message fell upon willing ears. It entered hearts full of the crusader's ardor, which had passed from men and entered the children. These gathered from near and from far. They could not be restrained. Of those kept by force at home, some sickened and died. The superstition of the age saw in their deaths the judgment of God upon those who had attempted to oppose the will of the Holy Spirit. Even the Pope feared to speak against the enterprise. The children of the poor went unattended. The rich sent servants with their little ones. Hundreds of monks joined the weird caravan. In July or August of the year forty thousand children, many of them under twelve, marched from Cologne. Some were clad in crusader's costume, white, with a cross of scarlet cloth upon the shoulder. Each wore a palmer's hat and bore a palmer's staff. They moved in two columns, their small hands grasping tiny pennons and mimic crosiers. Twenty thousand of them ascended the Rhine. They had no organization, no commissariat. Their only plan was to follow the leader, whom they believed to be inspired.

It seems to have been expected that they would be miraculously guarded. It almost seems as if they were.

At nightfall they lay down upon the grass and slept until the dawn. They ate what charity bestowed as they passed through village and hamlet. Those who had provisions in their small crusading sacks shared with those who had none. They advanced practising the hymns they were to sing before Jerusalem.

Some of these hymns which Nicholas had taught them are still preserved. One, if it was indeed composed by a boy of twelve, and not, as has been suspected, by his father, is little less than a miracle. Rendered from the Latin it runs thus: —

> "Fairest Lord Jesus,
> Ruler of all nations,
> Thou of Mary and of God the son!
> Thee will I cherish,
> Thee will I honor,
> Thee my soul's glory, joy, and crown.
>
> "Fair are the meadows,
> Fairer still the woodlands,
> Robed in the beauty of the spring!
> Jesus is fairer,
> Jesus is purer,
> Who makes our saddened hearts to sing."

They have reached the Alps. Hardship and famine have been at work. They are only ten thousand now. Still they struggle forward, over the terrible pass that nearly thwarted Hannibal and Napoleon.

Their tender feet press the flints and tread the ice of the lonely glacier, but the moon shines softly and the stars are bright while the little ones kneel at nightfall in the snow and their sobs pass into melody : —

> "Fair is the sunshine,
> Fairer still the moonlight,
> And the sparkling starry host!
> Jesus shines brighter,
> Jesus shines fairer,
> Than all the angels heaven can boast."

After seven hundred miles of journeying these little wanderers appear approaching Genoa. The amazed Italians ask the meaning of their coming.

"May we rest one night in your city? We are going to deliver Palestine and baptize the Paynim." The city asked the children to remain a few days for rest, and promised then to send them safely home. The offer was gently rejected.

"We would only rest one night in this city. To-morrow Jesus will make a path through the waters for his holy children, and we will journey on."

Bitter was their disappointment when the next day's sun revealed the ocean still impassible. Of these enthusiasts it is not known that one ever reached his home again. History has passed lightly over this marvellous episode as a mystery it is equally unable to explain or to deny.

The one truth preached by these children the world cannot afford to forget. It is that the harp is stronger than the sword. The crusades of the nineteenth century are between the rich and the poor. To bridge the space between them with genial fellowship has been a main work of Christmas.

Once a year, at the festival of Mithras, it is said that the Parthian monarch descended from his throne, stood upon the ground, clasped hand with the common people, and cried, " I am one of you." At the Saturnalia masters and slaves exchanged apparel, the masters served while the slaves sat at table. Liberty of speech was allowed. At the banquet some one was by vote elected temporary king. Beans, white and black, were used as ballots. White " yes," black " no." Generally a wit of obscure birth like Plautus was selected, and all his commands must be obeyed.

Hence the English Twelfth Night with its "King of the bean," or "Lord of Misrule." Here are germs of the old time English Christmas. Let the housemaid rise early on Christmas morning, for two village swains are waiting at the door. If the great sausage is not boiling over the fire at sunrise, they may take the damsel by her elbows between them, and run with her around the market-place till she is out of breath and ashamed of her laziness.

The centre of the Christmas dinner was the boar's-head, sacred animal, — because by rooting with his tusks in the ground he taught mankind to plough. It has been observed that this is not the only habit men appear to have derived from the same instructor. When the Puritans abolished the boar's-head by law, even the Christmas pie and plum-pudding were for a time counted heretical, which made Sir Roger de Coverly remark that he had hope of the Roundheads when he observed them at the king's pudding.

A beautiful dish was the peacock. Sometimes it was carefully skinned so as not to mar the plumage, the flesh cooked and replaced within the skin and brought upon the table with all the feathers flying. Sometimes it was baked in a pie, the head and tail in full splendor appearing above the crust, to give origin to the Shakespearian oath: " By the cock and pie."

In the third year of his reign King Henry VIII. celebrated Christmas at Greenwich. A castle was erected in the grand hall. Cannon frowned across the mimic moat. Knights armed cap-a-pie paced the battlements. On the pennon floating from the keep was written, " Castle Dangerous. "Before it appeared the king with five companions. They were clad in suits half velvet covered with gold spangles, half cloth of gold. They wore caps of russet satin embroidered with gold and brilliants. They charged upon the castle. Its pennon sank. The drawbridge was lowered. Forth came the defenders. They were the six most beautiful ladies of the court, clad in russet satin embroidered with leaves of gold and powdered with seed pearls. They danced a morris with the knights. Then the pennon rose again, and the fair dames led the knights captive within the castle.

Enormous sums were expended in such pageants by King Henry. But the revels were not confined to royalty. All classes participated. The bulwarks of rank were largely removed at Christmas time.

In the kitchen every member of the household from duke to scullion must aid in carrying the Yule log, while each one tried to drop his end upon his neighbor's toes, as Congressmen endeavor to carry through Congress bills which, though remunerative, are like to prove unpopular. Even the learned barristers must share in the revels. Dugdale tells us the matter was not left to their option. All the members of the bar were obliged to dance after the Christmas dinner, before the judges, chancellors, and benchers, and with them. "And this was thought very needful, as making these gentlemen more fit for their books at other times." In the reign of James I., all the barristers of Lincoln's Inn were disbarred by decimation, because they refused to dance at Candlemas according to the ancient order of the society. It would amaze us if Harvard should refuse to graduate students who could not or would not dance the hornpipe. Yet out of such soil grew Bacon, Burleigh, and Blackstone.

France seems least of all the nations in Europe to have enjoyed the spirit of Christmas. Frenchmen could not even make a Christmas pudding. Louis le Grand once attempted to regale the English ambassador upon that celebrated viand. He sent to London for the recipe, instructed the royal cook with his royal lips, told how to mingle the flour and the condiments, how many raisins and how much citron to use. But he forgot to tell the cook to boil the pudding in a bag, and the combined efforts of the greatest monarch, and the most famous *chef* in Europe resulted in a mess which had to be served like soup in a tureen, while the guests were compelled to harpoon the floating plums with forks or dredge them up with ladles.

The cynical, unlovely customs which have hung upon the robes of Christmas come from France. Such is April Fool's day, which was first devised in memory of the bootless errand on which Pilate sent Christ to Herod, and was afterwards transferred to the time of Easter.

At Christmastide the priests entered the pulpits and crowed as chanticleers, calling themselves St. Peter's cocks. They disguised, perhaps it would be more accurate to say revealed, themselves in asses' skins, and brayed in honor of Balaam, who first predicted the rising of the Star of Bethlehem. They celebrated the time, as that navigator who sighted certain bluffs in Southeastern Africa on Christmas Day, and therefore called them "Natal," or "birth town," without suspecting that they were the gateway to a land of diamonds. French merrymakings are more redolent of gas-lights than of May-blossoms. Frenchmen danced, but often in a fiendish style, — a style commemorated in that legend made familiar by the "Elegy of the Cork Leg."

A party of young people assembled near a church on the south of the Rhine to dance on Christmas Eve. A priest, disturbed at his devotions, asked them to desist. They refused. Three times he repeated the request. Three times they scornfully rejected it. He warned them to beware. They ridiculed his warning. On they danced. At last they grew weary. But as they would not stop when they could, now they could not when they would. The dawn broke, still they danced on. The town came to see. On they danced. The monk discerned his own sister in the cotillon. He seized her by the arm and tried to draw her from such fell companionship. Off came the arm in his hands, and the rest of her danced on. The ground was worn away to their ankles, then to their arm-pits. Their clothes fell off. Their ribs grew visible, their bones clattered like castanets; still they danced on twelve months, night and day, until at last Bishop Hubert took pity upon them, granted absolution, and they stopped.

Perhaps in no institution has the spirit of Christmas brotherhood gleamed more gayly than in the German Christmas fair. Let me show you one at Berlin. Six days before Christmas, a visible change passes over city and suburb. A magic change, as when the wand touched Cinderella, and the child of the ash-heap became the queen of the ballroom. The streets begin to be lined with fir-trees. The shop-windows grow kaleidoscopic. The central attraction is the Christmas fair. It is held in the royal square. Here a mimic city springs up in a night. The buildings are booths of fir boughs, and tents decked with evergreen. No monopolies are allowed. It is the people's fair. Peasants from the country are there, peddlers from the slums, princely merchants from the Linden. The booths are arranged in avenues that form a mimic town.

Each booth is adorned with prodigality of ornament, till it looks almost like a Christmas tree. At night wax tapers of countless colors gleam on every side. They are fastened in most surprising places, — hung upon twigs, thrust into pipe bowls, stuck into hat bands. All manner of articles are exposed for sale. Here is a pair of white china wolves lineally descended from the nurse of Romulus and Remus. There is the identical mouse which gnawed the lion free, whose biography is it not written in the chronicles of the book of Æsop? Blown glass fairies, gilt gingerbread ogres, plaster of Paris angels, wooden peacocks with bead eyes and chicken-feather tails, diminutive steamboats on wheels, disconsolate lovers done in sweet-cake with pathetic ditties in white sugar dropping from their lips; implacable furies on impossible dragons with red-foil eyes and tin claw toes; the bright faces of the damsels who offer these monsters for sale presenting sweet contrast to the monsters themselves.

The avenues are filled with a motley throng. Rich and poor are together here. The bright uniforms of the soldiers, the silver helmets of the police, harlequins fantastically clad, boys with colored lanterns and variegated transparencies. Some have rattles which they spring at you, and shriek with laughter as they see you start. One thinks himself at Rome in the carnival.

Woe to the spectator whose dignity rebukes the fun. At other times the Prussians are remarkable for the deference they show to rank and wealth. But to-night they effervesce. Here comes an elegant youth. From silken hat to mirror boot his attire is immaculate. Through his eye-glass he surveys the wild scene with the solemnity of a grasshopper on a light-house observing the ocean and seeming to wonder why it foams. A bright-eyed peasant girl casts tender glances toward him. He looks toward her booth. He pities her weakness. He will remind her that the wren must not too much admire the eagle. But he will not be cruel, for she blushes; poor child! He will buy a trifle. Alas for the young foreigner! He has yet to learn that buying trifles of young damsels at fairs is no trifle! What shall he buy? "Oh sir, this toilet box! See the cupid on the lid! Only five groschen, good sir, and a cupid on the lid!"

He pays the five groschen. "Thank you, kind sir, thank you!"

He tries to lift the lid, but it will not open.

"Let me show you, kind sir! Touch the little spring, kind sir."

He presses the spring: up flies the lid, forth darts a clawing demon with a terrific shriek, dashing a cloud of powder into his face. Peals of luscious laughter ripple around him, as blinking, sneezing, sputtering, his broadcloth ruined, he shouts for the police. There they stand, laughing also, for it is Christmas time, and this is the Christmas fair.

But the genius of kindness and Christmas polity is nowhere more completely presented than in the American conception of Santa Claus. I once knew a little boy who had seen that hero. It was after midnight when the child stole down the broad stairway, crossed the deserted hall, and entered the large dining-room. The fire was out. The moonlight cast fantastic shadows upon the floor, as he crouched beside the huge Franklin stove, shivering with cold and awe. A rustling in the chimney, a fall of soot upon the hearth. "He is coming! He is coming!"

"As still as death with stifled breath,"

the watching eyes dilate with fear and expectation. A moment of quivering excitement, and the fur cap, the twinkling eyes appear! But what is this? A tail! Bitter was the disappointment when there appeared the tame raccoon, which had been shut out by accident, and had taken this mode of entrance, not because it was Christmas but because it was cold. But the disappointment was tempered and made tolerable by the strong suspicion which the boy still retains, though thirty years have passed, that it was St. Nicholas, and that he suddenly changed into a familiar form to baffle and rebuke a wicked curiosity. Did not Proteus assume the appearance of a seal under similar conditions?

But why can Santa Claus enter only by the chimney? The road he travels was prepared by the Norse Goddess Hertha. At the festival held in her honor the house was decked with evergreens. An altar of flat stones, called Hertha's stones, contracted eventually into "hearthstone," was placed at one extremity of the hall in which the family assembled. Fir boughs were piled upon it, and the torch applied. As the crackling boughs shrivelled, the Goddess was supposed to descend through the smoke, and so to guide the flames that those skilled in Saga lore could predict the destinies of each person present from the movements of the fire flakes.

An irreverent spirit has suggested that these were not the only occasions on which the destinies of families have been known to be influenced by sparks.

When the older festival was absorbed in Christmas, Santa Claus must needs come by the way Hertha had opened for him.

St. Nicholas — the name has been contracted into Santa Claus by dropping the first instead of the last syllable, as Alexander is shortened into Sandy — must not be confounded, as he often is in America, with Kris-Kringle, the little Christ-child, or Christ-Kindlein, who goes about Holland on errands of loving-kindness. The veritable St. Nicholas was born at Patara early in the fourth century. His piety was unparalleled. His nurse could never wash the soles of his feet, because he would continually stand erect in the attitude of prayer, even while he was being bathed. His sanctity was so great that when an infant at the breast he fasted twice a week, and could not be induced to touch pap or gruel on Fridays. His virtues multiplied with his years, until he was known throughout Christendom as "The Good."

An Italian nobleman of wrecked fortunes had three daughters. Too poor to portion them with dowries, the wicked parent apprenticed them to degrading employments. St. Nicholas heard of this, came at night, and threw three bags filled with gold into the house, to be used as marriage portions for the girls, or returned to the giver. Thus he put the father in pawn for his children. This gave him rank as the first Christian pawnbroker. The three purses of gold, rounded into three gilded balls, which still hang above the doors of these benevolent institutions, and serve as stars to mariners, for the help of victims persecuted by the police, point to St. Nicholas as the patron saint of pawnbrokers.

The news of the saint's kindness was spread afar. The nuns of a certain convent begged their abbess to persuade St. Nicholas to visit them. He consented to do so, and sent word that every nun who gave him one of her stockings should receive it again filled with sweetmeats. Hence came his habit of filling stockings.

At another time a nobleman sent his two sons to Athens to be educated. But first he dispatched them to St. Nicholas to receive his blessing and advice. It was night when they reached the holy man's abode, and with boyish bashfulness they withdrew to the village inn to wait until the morning. There the landlord murdered them, stole their gold, and to conceal his crime chopped their bodies into small pieces, which he concealed in two barrels of salted meat. The deed was disclosed to St. Nicholas in a vision. He charged the innkeeper with the crime, brought him to confession and repentance, forgave him, resuscitated the defunct youths, sent them on their way rejoicing, and has been ever since the patron saint of schoolboys.

The legend of St. Nicholas is the protest of healthy human instinct against the ecclesiastical asceticism of the Middle Ages. That the wholesome reaction did not succeed without opposition may be, perhaps, inferred from the fact that the same conception, which we love to cherish by the name of Santa Claus, inspired in some minds those fears which are still suggested by that other name, "The Old Nic." But the wiser course prevailed. While the monks taught that piety and cheerfulness were foes, that the doors of heaven swung on leaden hinges, and that hilarity and gayety were crimes; in violent half-conscious protest against that accepted creed, the saintliest saint in all the calendar, the only one who never committed a sin, and whose saintship dates from his cradle, was sent forth in fullest sympathy with the universal human heart to scatter smiles and rain down gladness, and teach once more that only they who become as little children can enter the kingdom of God.

Thus Christmas bids us make our churches radiant, and our homes happy with the gladness children can enjoy. It is well worth our while to do so. Chambers quotes from Dr. Jamieson a letter of Hamilton's, written when the disciples of John Knox were striving to drive Christmas out of Scotland. The ministers, it is said, made their wives spin flax at the front doors, and the more zealous sent their servants into the fields to plough on Christmas Day, to emphasize their disapproval of the popular festivities. "Yes," wrote Hamilton, "the ministers of Scotland cause their wifis and servants to spin in open sight on Yule Day; and their auditors constrain their tenants to yoke their pleuchs on Yule Day in contempt of Christ's nativite! Whilk our Lord has not left unpunishit! For their oxen ran wod [mad] and brak their nekis, and lamit some o' the pleuch-men."

In our day there is small danger that such blunders will be repeated. He best uses Christmas who makes his home so happy that his children cannot be enticed from it. A happy childhood is a saving talisman through life. The angels that hover over his mother's chair follow a man always.

A youth sat in his solitary room thinking of the circle around his father's hearth. He was in a foreign land, it was the first Christmas he had spent away from home, and a huge city lay around him. In the great capital he thought no one but he seemed sad. The boy or the man who has grown too old to long for home is to be pitied, for home is the little mirror lake in this world, the only one that, by its still reflection of what bends over us, discloses the reality of heaven. The youth was homesick. There came a knock upon the door. A stranger entered. At least he was almost a stranger, for the two had met but once. The stranger brought an invitation to his house. Not without protest, for the young are often shy, the invitation was accepted. They did not go directly to the stranger's house. First, they made a little tour together. The stranger's pockets were plethoric, and he carried a large basket on his arm. It, too, was full. They went to many a door that had no bell, up many a stairway that was dark and dank. Wherever they appeared children clustered around them with gleeful welcomes. Each child received some token that Christ was in the world. For the sick there were delicacies, for the old comforts. When the youth praised the stranger's benevolence, the sole reply was this: "Oh, no! I am only trying to pay back!" The words were not quite plain, but both were made happy by sight of so many faces brightened by their coming, and sound of so many benedictions.

When pockets and basket were empty the two reached the stranger's house. There was waiting a little maiden just twelve months old to a day. A mother held her. The maiden crowed and cooed, pursed up her red lips to be kissed, and reached out her arms to be taken. Then by the light in her father's eyes the meaning grew plain of the words he had spoken: "Trying to pay back! Trying to pay back."

The memory of that Christmas has been to the youth who experienced it a perpetual benediction. He forgot that he was not one of the family. There were trifles upon the Christmas tree with his name written upon them. There was a chair for him at the Christmas table. When he feared for a moment he might jar the peace of the household by intrusion of foreign feet, the anxiety was banished by the echo of the words, "Trying to pay back!"

Perhaps the hostess divined the thought of her guest, for when they parted she said, with a grace of courtesy acquired by years of familiarity with courts and companionship with a queen, who has since become an empress, "When Noah opened the window and drew in the lonely and wing-weary dove it brought a leaf which made his family far more blessed than it found them."

In that Christmas Day the young man thought he saw a dim but lustrous reflection of that World to Come where a Happy New Year shall comfort those that mourn; where the Church of Christ shall appear without spot or wrinkle or any such thing; where praise and prayer shall be spontaneous as the carolling of larks; where all burdens shall be loosed and God's people shall find their joy in serving Him whose name is in their foreheads; where faith shall discern distinctly things not disclosed to sight; where Gideon's men shall rest from their enemies, Saul shall not seek the witches' cave, and Samson shall have learned the truth that can make him free; where the hearts of the children shall have been turned to their fathers, and the hearts of the fathers to their children, that the earth may not be smitten with a curse; where he that is least shall be greater than the greatest we have known; where none shall ask, " What must we do to be saved ? " but all shall be singing, " Thou wast slain and hast redeemed us to God by thy blood out of every kindred and tongue and nation ; " where all shall be filled with the Spirit of Him who left the bosom of his Father to make God manifest to men ; where the Unseen shall be recognized as the real; where the lesson of the lilies shall be heeded, the prophecies of Decoration Day fulfilled, and the gratitude which good men feel at Harvest Home find utterance in the psalm ascending with the voice of many waters, "Allelujah! for the Lord God Omnipotent reigneth. Let us rejoice and be glad and give honor to Him, for the marriage of the Lamb is come, and his wife hath made herself ready!"

www.ingramcontent.com/pod-product-compliance
Lightning Source LLC
Chambersburg PA
CBHW030806230426
43667CB00008B/1085